D1623968

231.8 W617w   [30034]

Whitney, Barry L.

What are they saying about
 God and evil?

DATE DUE

MEMPHIS UNIVERSITY SCHOOL
HYDE LIBRARY
6191 PARK AVENUE
MEMPHIS, TENNESSE 38119-5399

DEMCO

WHAT ARE THEY SAYING ABOUT
GOD AND EVIL?

What Are They Saying About God and Evil?

Barry L. Whitney

PAULIST PRESS
New York/Mahwah

Acknowledgements
The Publisher gratefully acknowledges the use of excerpts from *Encountering Evil,* edited by Stephen T. Davis, Copyright 1981 by John Knox Press, used by permission.

Copyright © 1989
by Barry L. Whitney

All rights reserved. No part of this book may be reproduced or transmitted in any form or by any means, electronic or mechanical, including photocopying, recording or by any information storage and retrieval system without permission in writing from the publisher.

Library of Congress Cataloging-in-Publication Data

Whitney, Barry L.
    What are they saying about God and evil? / Barry L. Whitney.
      p.   cm.
    Bibliography: p.
    ISBN 0-8091-3078-5 : $5.95 (est.)
    1. Theodicy.   I. Title.
  BT 160.W526   1989   89-30728
  231'.8—dc19   CIP

Published by Paulist Press
997 Macarthur Boulevard
Mahwah, N.J. 07430

Printed and bound in the
United States of America

231.8
W617w

Contents

30034

Hyde Library
Memphis University School

Dedication

to
Christopher Jón,
Matthew Pétur,
and Barbara Lára

May you find the knowledge and strength
to endure the adversities
which inevitably will come.

1
Introduction:
The Problem of Evil

We live in a world of unprecedented atheism, humanism and despair. Ours is a world where belief in God certainly is not easy to maintain. The growth of modern science over the past few centuries has given rise to an explanation of the world which challenges traditional religious beliefs, for science purports to explain all things in terms of natural causes (i.e., in terms of "physics and chemistry"). Science, as such, has "no need for the theistic hypothesis," as the scientist LaPlace supposedly once informed France's Emperor Napoleon.

The scientific challenge to theism is monumental, and yet there is an even more urgent problem for the theist: the problem of reconciling belief in God with the world's suffering and anguish. In the minds of many theologians, this is by far the most serious threat to religious belief, a threat which the contemporary scientific alternative has rendered more pressing than ever. How can we believe in an all-powerful and all-loving God who orders and guides our lives, when all around us there exists such devastating evil and suffering? Could an all-powerful God not have eliminated the suffering and pain we creatures must endure? Should an

1

all-powerful and all-loving God not have done so? Indeed, could an all-powerful and all-loving God not have created a better world in the first place, a world with less evil or perhaps with none at all?

This, in brief, is the infamous "problem of evil," technically referred to as "theodicy."[1] It has been a major concern of theologians for centuries and persists as one of the most perplexing and disconcerting of problems. It not only is a problem, moreover, for professional theologians and philosophers, but has been a prevalent theme in poetry, novels, drama and in other facets of human creativity and inquiry. "Everywhere, everywhen, and everyhow, it seems, this problem has been near the heart of the important work of significant writers,"[2] artists, and others. The problem of evil is a problem which no human being can ignore; it is, as the late theologian Karl Rahner pointed out, "universal, universally oppressive, and {a problem which} touches our existence at its very roots."[3]

The problem of evil certainly is not restricted to Christians, although the limitations of this present book must confine the discussion of the issue to the Christian perspective. Christianity shares with Judaism and Islam a uniquely formulated problem of evil inasmuch as these three "western religions" seek to reconcile the existence of evil with belief in one God (monotheism). Other religions, which believe in the existence of many gods (polytheism), or in the existence of no gods at all (as is the case, for example, with early Buddhism and Jainism), are faced with a radically different problem of evil. Christians, Jews and Muslims must face the challenge of reconciling belief in one God, the creator of all things *ex nihilo* ("out of nothing"), with the devastating reality of evil and suffering in the world. The three western religions cannot appeal to evil gods as the source of this misery nor transpose the issue to a non-theistic level.[4]

(i) The Formulation of the Problem of Evil

The Christian problem of evil has been formulated over the centuries by philosophers and theologians in a fairly consistent manner. Yet perhaps the most succinct and renowned articulation is to be found in the writings of the eighteenth century philosopher, David Hume: "Is he {God} willing to prevent evil, but not able? then is he impotent. Is he able, but not willing? then is he malevolent. Is he both able and willing? whence then is evil?"[5] Hume considered evil to be decisive evidence against the existence of God[6] and a significant number of contemporary writers concur, many of whom have focused upon the apparent logical inconsistencies inherent in the Humean triad of propositions.[7]

It is not only skeptics, however, who formulate the theodicy problem in this way. Christian theologians do likewise, yet without acquiescing to the atheistic conclusion. C. S. Lewis, to cite one prominent example, began his inquiry into the theodicy riddle as follows: "If God were good, He would wish to make His creatures perfectly happy and if God were almighty He would be able to do what He wished. But the creatures are not happy. Therefore, God lacks either goodness or power, or both."[8] Philosopher Nelson Pike likewise writes:

> If God is omnipotent, then He could prevent evil if He wanted to. And if God is perfectly good, then He would want to prevent evil if He could. Thus, if God exists and is both omnipotent and perfectly good, then there exists a being who *could* prevent evil if he wanted to and who would *want to* prevent evil if he *could*. And if this last is true, how can there be so many evils in the world?[9]

The question is clear: "*Si deus est, unde malum?*" ("If God exists, why is there evil?")

(ii) Moral and Physical Evil

The problem of evil is discussed most often as two separate (though interrelated) problems. What is the reason, we ask, for *moral evil*?; and why does the world contain *physical evil*?

"Moral evil" can be defined as "sin" or, more simply perhaps, as the evil caused by human beings: the greed, conceit, cruelty, rage, contempt, and countless other means by which we so relentlessly torment ourselves and our fellow human beings. Saint Augustine (354–430 A.D.) believed that *all* of the evil in the world could be attributed to this one source: the misuse of our free will. More precisely, he taught that human sin is the cause of moral evil and that physical evil is God's just punishment for our moral evil.[10]

Augustine's explanation for physical evil (as divine punishment) has been challenged, as we shall see, yet many contemporary theologians do agree with Augustine that it is reasonable to suppose that *most* of the world's evil is, in fact, brought about by human beings themselves. C. S. Lewis, for example, estimated that four-fifths of evil originates in human wickedness, and theologian John Hick has insisted that "by far the greatest bulk of human suffering is due either wholly or in part to the actions and inactions of other human beings." Saint Thomas Aquinas proposed much the same[11] and it does seem to be a suggestion which has great force. The disgusting inhumanity human beings display toward one another, to say nothing of our wanton and disgraceful callousness with regard to lesser life forms and to the environment, most certainly leads to incalculable destruction and misery.

In his classic presentation of the problem of evil, David Hume has listed with alarming precision the seemingly endless variety of moral evils with which we human beings mutually torment ourselves: the "oppression, injustice, contempt, contumely, violence, sedition, war, calumny, treachery, {and} fraud," etc. Consider also the "remorse, shame, anguish, rage, disappointment, anxiety, fear, dejection, despair—who has ever passed through life without cruel inroads from these tormentors?"[12]

Yet perhaps no one has documented human cruelty more vividly than the great nineteenth century Russian novelist, Feodor Dostoevski, in his masterpiece, *The Brothers Karamazov*.[13] His heart-rending accounts of the vicious sufferings inflicted upon children not only by strangers, but (so often) by their own parents, numb and offend our sensibilities. A child of five, for example, was kicked and tortured by her parents until her body was one bruise, and she then was locked up in a cold and frosty outhouse for wetting the bed. That innocent child wept alone in the dark, crying to her loving God to protect her, and while she cried and prayed, her parents slept soundly, apparently oblivious to her anguish. We all know that such cruelties to defenseless children continue to be a fact of life, and that this kind of abuse is only one instance of our race's seemingly infinite propensity for the mental and physical cruelty by which we misuse and abuse our powers of free will.

Just as devastating and most certainly as disturbing is the "physical" (or "natural") evil we creatures must endure: the birth defects, the seemingly infinite assortment of diseases which afflict us, the squalor and malnutrition, and the devastation caused by apparently arbitrary forces of nature, the misnamed "acts of God," which wreak such terrible havoc: the droughts and famines, the hurricanes and tornadoes, the floods and volcanoes, and countless other "natural disasters." Jesuit scholar G. H. Joyce has written pointedly about the seriousness of this problem: "The actual amount of suffering which the human race endures is immense," he notes, "and if we focus our attention upon the miseries of life we may be led to wonder how God came to deal so harshly with His creatures as to provide them with such a home."[14]

David Hume's time-honored description of natural evils argues a similar point, and while his account may be somewhat overstated, for many people its truth is all too evident:

> The whole earth . . . is cursed and polluted. A perpetual war is kindled amongst all living creatures. Necessity, hunger, want stimulate the strong and courageous; fear, anxiety, terror agitate the weak and infirm. The first entrance into life gives anguish to the newborn infant and to its wretched parent; weakness, impotence, distress attend each stage of that life, and it is, at last, finished in agony and horror.[15]

The issue before us is clear: how can we continue to *worship*, indeed how can we even *believe* in the existence of an almighty and all-loving God, when the world is so ravaged by evils and misery? The question cannot be avoided, whether we seek a rational, theological explanation or whether, as suffering people, we attempt merely to cope with the evils and tragedies which devastate our lives, evils which so often come with crushing swiftness, with little or no warning, and which leave no life untouched.

(iii) Faith and Reason

Discussions of the theodicy issue generally make a crucial distinction between what is known as the "faith solution" and the intellectual (or rational) solutions, the latter referred to as "theodicies." The faith solution cautions us that human beings never will comprehend fully the reasons *why* God permits (or perhaps causes) the world's evil, but that since we believe in the existence of God, we ought to place our faith and trust in the belief that there is a good and just reason for evil, a reason which forever may be known only to God. Human attempts to uncover this reason (or reasons) not only are wasted efforts, proponents of the faith solution are quick to warn us, but, more seriously, any such efforts to unravel this divine mystery smack of impiety and (perhaps) even blasphemy.

The faith solution is assessed critically in *Chapter 2*: its strengths are acknowledged, and then some of its most serious weaknesses are exposed. The remainder of the book addresses the rational solutions. *Chapter 3* discusses the writings of some prominent contemporary biblical scholars who are investigating biblical insights into the issue. *Chapter 4* explores the contemporary Augustinian-Thomistic solution, the "traditional" theodicy which has dominated Christian thinking for hundreds of years. The next four chapters present some of the novel insights which have been proposed by modern Irenaean thinkers, notably John Hick (*Chapter 5*), by process theologians (*Chapter 6*) and finally by a number of other contemporary theologians and philosophers (*Chapter 7 and Chapter 8*). The final chapter concludes this study.

2
The Faith Solution
and Its Difficulties

Theologian John Hick, in my opinion, undeniably is correct in his observation that it is the believer in God, more so than the skeptic, who is forced to come to terms with the problem of evil. For it is the believer who claims that the situation is other than it appears; it is the believer who insists that despite the evil and suffering in the world, an all-powerful and all-loving God *does* exist[1] and that there must be a "morally sufficient reason" why God would permit evil.[2]

What this reason is, however, appears forever to be beyond the grasp of human understanding. The most obvious course of action for the believer, accordingly, is to seek to cultivate an attitude of trusting faith in God, despite the preponderance of evil and misery in the world. The "faith solution" recommends precisely this stance, and rejects as fruitless and impious any intellectual attempt to explain God's ways to humanity. The Book of Job (see *Chapter 3*) is a classic presentation of this perspective. The faith stance it recommends has persisted strongly and unabated throughout the centuries.

(i) The Appeal of the Faith Solution

The undeniably persuasive attraction of the faith solution lies in the fact that it represents an amazingly simple solution to the problem of evil and that it provides an appealing reassurance and comfort to believers who otherwise might succumb to their suffering in despair. Thus, Karl Rahner, as we shall see, rejected as inadequate the traditional intellectual attempts to answer the theodicy question, pointing out that we must learn to accept the "incomprehensibility of suffering" as "part of the incomprehensibility of God."[3] In Rahner's view, God allows evil for a reason known only to God: "the true answer must be only the incomprehensibility of God in his freedom and nothing else."[4]

Process theologian John Cobb has advocated much the same: as we all struggle to cope with the world's evil and suffering, he suggests, we must never lose touch with the faith which is so vital and necessary to sustain us: "We cannot believe in God unless we experience life as a blessing. We cannot experience life as a blessing if we have no hope. We cannot have hope unless we believe in God. We need all three. . . . We must not let our sense of outrage destroy our belief in the goodness of life."[5]

This same theme runs through the writings of mystic Simone Weil:

Affliction makes God appear to be absent for a time, more absent than a dead man, more absent than light in the utter darkness of a cell. A kind of horror submerges the whole soul. During this absence there is nothing to love. What is terrible is that if, in this darkness where there is nothing to love, the soul ceases to love, God's absence becomes final. The soul has to go on wanting to love. . . . Then, one day, God will come to show himself to this soul and reveal the beauty of the world to it, as in the case of Job. But if the soul stops loving it falls, even in this life, into something almost equivalent to hell.[6]

The Easter message, I would suggest, could be interpreted in a way which confirms her point: amid the confusion and despair in losing their beloved master, the faith of the disciples was rewarded with an experience of the resurrected Jesus as the Christ. The same point, of course, is prevalent also in the Book of Job: despite Job's intense suffering and anguish, his faith, which had been tested so severely, in fact was rewarded in the end.

Theologian Paul Schilling has documented some remarkable testimonies of the captivating power of the faith solution, contemporary illustrations which reveal how faith holds together lives which otherwise would collapse in numbing despair. One example is that of the priest, Père Albert Jamme, who, after thirty-five years of laboring seven days a week to collect and painstakingly translate some rare manuscripts, lost much of his life's work in a tragic fire. Jamme's response was to state: "I know there is a great lesson in this. But I don't know what it is. What He {God} wanted me to learn, I do not know. That He had a reason, there is no doubt."[7]

(ii) Difficulties with the Faith Solution

There can be no question that the ultimate reason for evil will remain forever beyond human comprehension: finite human minds are unlikely ever to comprehend fully this great mystery. The faith stance, accordingly, is an appealing, inevitable and reasonable response. Its captivating force lies in the fact that it offers a genuine comfort and a considerably satisfying consolation that all things happen for a reason, a reason known (and perhaps ordained) by God. Yet, as many theologians have pointed out, the faith solution is not without difficulties, difficulties which seriously jeopardize its viability and usefulness in the lives of suffering people. To a consideration of some of these problems we now turn.

In his admirable presentation of the theodicy problem, Paul Schilling has pointed out that the faith solution all-too-easily *can* lead to a *mesmerizing fatalism* which rationalizes away any human responsibility for evil.[8] It may be comforting and reassuring to find meaning and significance in daily events by attributing all goods and evils to divine providence; yet such an attitude often produces a destructive resignation, fatalism, and a numbing despair that we have no genuine control over our lives. The faith solution, in short, may encourage us to abdicate our moral and social responsibilities, for if we really believe that the evils and apparent injustices in the world are the consequences of God's incomprehensible plan, we may well be led into an attitude of social inactivity and a lack of serious concern for the sufferings of others. The poor and the wretched indeed will be with us always, as Jesus stated, yet this may be so largely because we have been content for so long to believe that we are not responsible for earthly events, believing rather that all things are part of the divine plan.

The faith stance, moreover, not only can inculcate this deplorable attitude in us, but it must be conceded that it is *an unrealistic option* for many people. We cannot expect, quite frankly, that calling upon suffering people to "have faith" in God's providential care will be helpful for many people, since it is often this very suffering which retards their potential openness to faith and hope. This is all the more true for those reflective Christians who feel a sincere obligation to strengthen their spirituality by seeking a

deeper understanding—rather than mere blind acceptance—of their religious beliefs. Such people take seriously
the commandment of Jesus that we love God not only with
our hearts and souls, but also with our minds.

Serious intellectual reflection about our religious
beliefs is anything but impious, despite those who would so
condemn it. Informed study and reflection is an essential
aspect of religious commitment for many people, for it is a
task which enhances and significantly deepens faith.
Indeed, it seems that serious reflection is indispensable for
religiously mature people if faith is to remain an active part
of our lives.

This is not to deny that the ability of many people to
maintain a strong and unquestioning belief in God, despite
evil and suffering, is commendable and enviable; yet ultimately such faith is blind and uninformed, often leading
easily into a fanaticism and into a narrow and intolerant
dogmatism. It may *seem* impious to inquire into the mystery of suffering, yet faith "does not automatically turn the
uncertainties of life into certainties" (as the physicist-theo-
logian Ian Barbour has pointed out in his useful discussion
of this point).[9] Faith must be supported with rational thinking, for only in this way can a blind faith become a more
mature and critical faith, a faith which may be far more
able to withstand the vicissitudes of evil and suffering.

The inspiring and well-known testimony of C. S. Lewis
is a classic example of the point at issue. After writing about
the theodicy problem from a purely theoretical stance in his
book, *The Problem of Pain*, Lewis experienced the bitter
and tragic loss of his wife. His account of the grief he
endured and the search he underwent to find a more meaningful and mature faith is documented in another of his
books, *A Grief Observed*, published after his own death.

It is instructive to notice that, in his extreme grief,
Lewis rejected the traditional forms of comfort: (i) his for-

mer faith seemed irrelevant: "You never know how much you really believe," he wrote, "until its truth or falsehood becomes a matter of life and death to you. . . . Apparently the faith—I thought it faith—which enables me to pray for the other dead has seemed strong only because I have never really cared, not desperately, whether they existed or not. Yet I thought I did";[10] (ii) the faith of his consoling friends also seemed inconsequential: "don't come talking to me," he writes, "about the consolations of religion or I shall suspect that you don't understand";[11] and (iii) he rejects as trivial the comfort of Scripture and rebuts Saint Paul's exhortation, "Do not mourn like those that have no hope," with the anguished and bitter retort: "It astonishes me, the way we are invited to apply to ourselves words so obviously addressed to our betters. What St. Paul says can comfort only those who love God better than the dead, and the dead better than themselves."[12]

(iii) Understanding and Coping with Evil

Discussions of the problem of evil ought to acknowledge (but often do not) that there are two distinct types of questions involved. One is referred to as the "existential" problem; the other, as the "theoretical" problem.[13] The former focuses upon how we can *cope* with the anguish and misery in the world, while the latter seeks to formulate ever more comprehensive and viable *rational solutions* to the problem of evil. The faith solution is closely intertwined with the existential issue, and this may contribute to a further and significant difficulty with it. I shall elaborate.

For many people, the existential perspective is primary, a fact which certainly is understandable since the theoretical question does not appear to be as urgent nor as pressing as the day by day struggle to cope with the pain and suffering we must all endure. John Bowker, accordingly, in his *Problems of Suffering in Religions of the World*, writes that there "is nothing theoretical or abstract about it {theodicy}. To talk of suffering is to talk not of an academic problem but of the sheer bloody agonies of existence."[14]

Human beings, by necessity, have learned to cope in an incredibly varied and imaginative number of ways, as Brian Hebblethwaite's recent book, *Evil, Suffering, and Religion*,[15] so aptly illustrates. Among the most popular and effective coping techniques he discusses are such strategies as the *renunciation or rejection of the world*, which for Christians takes the form of *repentance*; *seeking mystical knowledge* through a variety of meditative techniques; *religious worship*; *performing morally valuable acts*; and coping through *sacrifice*, including altruistic self-sacrificing for the good of others.

This existential or practical response to the theodicy issue often focuses upon the God of salvation who acts decisively to overcome evil. Dorothee Soelle, in her notable book, *Suffering*, has addressed this point, criticizing the apathy which so often characterizes human responses to evil and exposing the fact that "all suffering is social suffering." Soelle calls for more active opposition to all forms of human oppression. Yet God shares in our suffering, she insists, and it is in our suffering that we participate in the suffering of Christ.[16]

Jürgen Moltmann, in his seminal book, *The Crucified God*, has pursued this theme: the crucial issue of theodicy lies in God's salvific activity to overcome evil.[17] Moltmann characterizes God as a fellow-sufferer (see *Chapter 8*), but, unlike Soelle, insists that the deity takes our suffering into the very Godhead: "The misery that we cause and the unhappiness that we experience are {God's} misery and unhappiness. Our history of suffering is taken up into his history of suffering."[18]

In another of his influential books, *Theology of Hope*, Moltmann assures us that evil will be overcome and transfigured by God, but only at the end of history.[19] We shall "be taken, without limitations and conditions, into the life and suffering, the death and resurrection of God, and in faith {we shall participate} . . . corporeally in the fullness of God. There is nothing that can exclude {us} from the situation of God."[20] The only answer for suffering people, then, as one of Moltmann's commentators points out, "is God's redemptive deed on the cross. For faith, it is this very deed which allows the word of liberation and succour to be spoken and heard."[21]

The other means of dealing with the problem of evil, however, is considered by many theologians to be just as critical, if indeed not *more* so, than this emphasis upon eschatological hope and practical coping techniques. Rather than appealing to what God is doing to overcome evil or, indeed, to what we can do to cope with evil, the theoretical question asks, quite bluntly, whether belief in God is compatible with the reality of evil in the world. I have suggested that this question is of primary importance, and while finite human minds never will uncover a full and completely satisfying explanation, the need to ask the question and to seek answers seems to be inescapable: we can *cope* with evil far better if we have some *understanding*, however tentative and oblique, of its relationship to God.

It is regrettable that so many Christians (here, we are not referring to the professional theologians) face their suffering with little else than blind faith in God and with a largely uninformed, makeshift set of solutions. Such pious and sincere faith most assuredly is not to be ridiculed nor demeaned, but it could become a much stronger and far more mature faith if it were to appropriate some of the insights offered by serious theological reflection upon the theodicy question (and, indeed, upon other religious matters). Coping with evil, in short, could be enhanced greatly by theological reflection upon the problem of evil, rather than merely accepting the fact of evil, or indeed even by working actively to eradicate it. We must learn to cope with evil, but just as surely we must try to answer the question as to *why* it exists and how it is related to the will of God.

This undoubtedly is what John Hick had in mind in urging us to seek some semblance of an intellectual perspective on this issue, as much as we are capable of attaining.[22] It may well be that rational reflection "cannot profess to create faith," but, rather, can only "preserve an already existing faith from being overcome by this dark mystery"; and "even if no complete theodicy is possible, certain approaches to it may be less inadequate than others, and it may thus be possible to reach some modest degree of genuine illumination upon the subject and to discover helpful criteria by which to discriminate among speculations concerning it."[23]

Michael Peterson, in his book, *Evil and the Christian God*, has addressed this point. Despite countless authors who are content to treat the problem of evil as purely "emotional,"[24] Peterson's point is that the emotional component tends to aim "at little more than inducing certain subjective states. . .: resignation, hope, courage, or whatever," and when such "emotional considerations take precedence over rational ones, spontaneous answers given in the face of actual evils are usually fragmentary and inapplicable, and ultimately become arbitrary and relative."[25] A faith, in other words, which is uninformed by rational reflection is inadequate: "The classic and enduring problem concerns the rational acceptability of Christian belief in light of the evil in the world, regardless of how different persons respond emotionally to the various evils which they encounter."[26] To an exploration of the rational study of the theodicy issue we now turn for the remainder of this book.

3
Contemporary Biblical Theodicy

In the previous chapter, we pointed out that many people continue to cope with evil and suffering by seeking to preserve an active and trusting faith that God loves and cares for us all, despite the pain and anguish which God apparently permits or perhaps even causes. Many Christians, moreover, not only seek to sustain their belief in the existence and care of a loving God, but this belief often takes the form of an unquestioning faith in the Bible. The Bible is for Christians, after all, an inspired revelation which, among other things, contains numerous explanations for the world's evil.

Biblical scholars are aware, however (as Daniel Simundson, for example, has noted in a recent book, *Faith Under Fire*),[1] that the Bible offers "no single, clear-cut" answer, no systematic solution to the problem of evil. Erhard Gerstenberger, moreover, in his highly respected book on biblical theodicy, *Suffering*, co-authored with Wolfgang Schrage, attributes this lack of success (with respect to the Old Testament writers) "in finding an unequivocal answer to the question of how we are to think of the relationship of the one God of Israel to suffering," as an "indifference toward problems of theory and structure."[2]

Schrage informs us that the same holds for the New Testament writers: the fact that there are a multiplicity of solutions offered is itself "a warning against absolutizing one of them or trying to bring them all together into a harmonized system."[3]

The biblical solutions may be characterized in many ways, but perhaps the most fundamental distinction to be noted is that the Bible contains passages which assume, on the one hand, a divine determinism of earthly events and, on the other hand, that creaturely freedom is the cause of evil and suffering.[4] Needless to say, many scholars have commented that these two views are paradoxical and ambiguous at best, and incoherent and incompatible at worst. God's sovereign power must be maintained, for this is an essential Christian belief; yet the issue has been to comprehend this divine causal agency in a way which does not destroy the authenticity and genuine viability of creaturely freedom.

In an important and provocative book, *Divine Sovereignty and Human Responsibility*, D. A. Carson has addressed this issue under the rubric of divine sovereignty and human responsibility, a book which is indebted (among others) to E. P. Sanders' majestic and seminal book, *Paul and Rabbinic Judaism*.[5] Carson focuses mainly upon the Gospel of John but considers also the relevant Old Testament and inter-testamental sources (the latter including the Apocrypha and pseudepigrapha, the Dead Sea Scrolls, targums and rabbinic literature). His thesis is that while the aforementioned texts often juxtapose divine sovereignty and human responsibility, they manifest very little awareness of, or concern with, the theoretical difficulties which have been so important in the writings of historical and contemporary thinkers. In those passages where the ancient writers *do* seek to address the issue somewhat (as in Job, Ecclesiastes, Habakkuk, and others), "their interest is focused on a practical area, viz. how to reconcile God's goodness and power and elective purposes with the vicissitudes they actually experience."[6]

The apocalyptic literature and the New Testament writings are much the same, although Carson shows that there has been an historical progression in the level of tension between divine causation and human freedom. This issue has been a perennial problem in the history of Christian thought, but Carson insists that the tension is not one which can be resolved. Both divine sovereignty and human responsibility must be acknowledged: while most biblical writers "presuppose human responsibility," he holds, "they not only presuppose divine sovereignty but insistently underscore it, even when the devastations of observable phenomena appear to fly in the face of such belief."[7]

This juxtaposition of human freedom with divine causative control, however, has led theologians (more often than not) to overshadow our freedom by emphasizing divine sovereign power.[8] It is this ancient understanding of God which provides the fundamental rationale behind the biblical solutions to the theodicy question: these explanations are, in short, attempts to clarify *why* God allows evil and suffering in the world. The basic assumption is that God allows or directly causes human suffering for a morally justifiable reason: perhaps we are being punished for our sins; perhaps our faith is being tested; perhaps we are being disciplined or warned; perhaps our sufferings are a means to bring about certain goods in the world, as did the redemptive suffering of Christ; and so on.

To a fuller look at some of these proposed explanations for evil we now shall turn. Later, we shall discuss the important perspective of many contemporary scholars who reject this dominant biblical understanding of a God who allows (or, indeed, causes) evil for some supposedly good—although ultimately incomprehensible—reason. For centuries, the theodicy question has been asking *why* God *permits* or *causes* evil; but many contemporary theologians insist that this question is wholly inappropriate as a starting point for the problem of evil. The very question is misdirected, they suggest, and by implication the answers likewise are fallacious.

(i) Adam and Eve

Despite the fact that many Christian laypeople understand the Bible to be, more or less, a literal (scientifically and historically accurate) account, theological scholarship has cautioned against this interpretation. Bultmann's celebrated "demythologizing" of the biblical record makes this point, and James Barr's recent writings on the shortcomings of a fundamentalist interpretation of the biblical record have been widely read and highly acclaimed.[9]

The Genesis story of Adam and Eve is particularly relevant to this issue, since the Genesis text has been utilized heavily in traditional accounts as the main explanation for the origin of evil in a world which otherwise would have remained a utopic paradise. It attributes evil to the "fall" of the first human pair and, consequently, to the misguided choices of their tainted progeny. This explanation was to become the dominant teaching about evil in the Old Testament world and it was confirmed in the influential writings of St Paul. Since then, it has gained a central and privileged place in "virtually all subsequent Christian thought concerning sin and evil."[10]

Contemporary biblical scholars realize, of course, that the biblical story of the fall contains primary and indispensable religious truths. They tell us, however, that these truths are expressed in culturally conditioned language and, as such, the words used to express the religious truths should not be taken literally. A loving God is the creative power behind all reality—this is perhaps the main religious truth contained in the story—yet biblical research over the past two hundred years has concluded that the language used in the biblical creation account is far from scientifically accurate. The language is replete with metaphor, symbol and myth. A recent book by S. D. Fohr, *Adam and Eve: The Spiritual Symbolism of Genesis and Exodus*,[11] has illustrated this point exceptionally well.

If we consider also the findings of modern science over the past few centuries, furthermore, we gain an additional confirmation of the non-literal nature of much[12] of the biblical accounts. Scientific evolution has no place for an historical Adam and Eve, and yet the very foundation of the traditional solution to the problem of evil rests upon belief in the "fall" into sin of the first human pair. There have always been serious theological problems in attributing evil and suffering to the fall of Adam and Eve (how, for example, could such good creatures sin in the first place?), but now that biblical scholarship no longer takes the story of the fall literally, the very basis of the principal Christian solution to the theodicy issue is seriously undermined. New approaches are being investigated by many contemporary scholars.

(ii) Satan

There are other biblical solutions to the theodicy problem which also are being explored in light of the current theological situation. A literal interpretation of those biblical passages which attribute evil and suffering to Satan and his cohorts, however, is not a popular view among the overwhelming majority of academic theologians. Biblical passages which refer to Satan (the creation and fall accounts of Genesis, in particular) are interpreted mythologically and symbolically by contemporary theologians. There are notable exceptions,[13] to be sure; yet, as Schilling points out, "theologians have sought since the Enlightenment to demythologize the devil, rejecting his personal presence and viewing him rather as a symbol of the ever-present power of evil in human life."[14] It is mainly the conservative evangelical Christians who continue to interpret the Bible literally and who affirm the literal existence of Satan.

Satan, of course, has had a long and interesting history within biblical thought and in the subsequent Christian tradition. He is the "angel of Yahweh" (Nm 22:22) who sets himself up as an "opposer" to Balaam. He patrols the earth and reports human offenses to God (Job 1:6–12; Ps 109:6; Zech 3:1–2; 1 Chr 21:1). In post-exilic times, he has become a bad angel who "tempts" human beings and seeks to bring about our destruction. He is identified also as the serpent in paradise (Wis 2:24). In the New Testament, likewise, Satan (also called Beelzebub, Belial, the evil one, the accuser, the adversary, the enemy, etc.) is conceived as a fallen angel (Lk 10:18) and as the great enemy of God who tempts humans to evil and deceit (Mt 4:3; 1 Thes 3:5; 1 Cor 7:5; Jn 8:44) and who causes various calamities. In post-biblical tradition, moreover, Satan's depiction as an evil power remains a dominant popular belief, sustained not only by official church doctrine but by literary classics like Milton's *Paradise Lost*, Goethe's *Faust*, and Byron's *Cain*. Recent movies depicting Satan and exorcisms indicate that belief in Satan as a personal power has survived into this century.[15]

This question of Satan's actual or symbolic existence, nevertheless, is not the primary one to be faced. For even if Satan is an actual being, the theodicy question would remain unresolved. Belief in the existence of an evil power leads quickly into a dualistic religion, a dualism which contradicts the essence of Christian monotheistic belief: Christians believe that there is one God who created all things, and it is irrelevant, therefore, whether or not Satan is an actual entity, since the positing of this evil power as being responsible for the world's evil merely transports the question to a transcendental realm of speculation, as Schilling contends,[16] and certainly does not answer the central question as to *why* God would permit evil, through Satan or otherwise.

(iii) Divine Punishment, Retribution and Discipline

The extremely popular and influential view that evil is explained as divine punishment, or as divine discipline, remains prevalent among many biblical scholars. The fact that the word "pain" is derived from the Latin word "poena," meaning "punishment," is not coincidental, but points to the predominant influence which has been afforded to the divine punishment explanation for evil.

The biblical record undeniably contains countless references to evil as the direct consequence of divine punishment[17] and divine discipline;[18] and yet, while these explanations of evil and suffering have been exploited heavily, there are a significant number of biblical passages themselves which dispute the premise of these views (that God causes evil for such reasons). Some influential biblical scholars, furthermore, have disputed rather forcefully the divine punishment theme in the biblical texts. Klaus Koch, for example, has analyzed the biblical passages which seem to make the case for divine retribution most strongly in the Old Testament and has argued that they do not, in fact, support the traditional interpretations.[19]

Walter Brueggemann has extended Koch's analysis to consider the Old Testament's theodicy in its social dimension.[20] Others, like James Crenshaw, are arguing that the doctrine of divine retribution places inappropriately severe limits upon God's power.[21] Still others argue that the divine punishment solution suggests a rather primitive view of God as one who continually intervenes in worldly affairs to reward the good and punish the evil-doers. The seemingly arbitrary and unfair distribution of evil and suffering certainly counts against this view.[22]

(iv) Divine Warnings and Tests of Faith

There are many biblical passages which explain evil as a divine warning or a test of faith, given by God explicitly for these purposes.[23] This certainly was the case with Job whose physical and mental torments were a test of his faith, a faith which served the moral end, if not of bringing him back to the path of righteousness (for he supposedly already was righteous, according to the myth), at least of bringing him to a much clearer acknowledgement of God's great power and glory, and to a further strengthening of his powers of faith and the ability to resist evil. Paul, likewise, saw his suffering as a test of faith, a call to remain steadfast and patient (2 Cor 8:2).

Many scholars, however, have cautioned that this explanation for evil must be utilized with care. Crenshaw argues that divine testing must *not* be seen (as it is all-too-often) in isolation from divine pathos.[24] Others stress even more strongly that the issue here is one which centers upon an inadequate representation of God's power vis-à-vis human free will. Is it appropriate to attribute evil to the causal agency of God for *any* reason? Suffering can be *used* and *understood* as a test of faith; this much is granted. But to hold that God deliberately caused the evil for this or any other reason (as a warning, perhaps), may well presuppose a fallacious and inadequate understanding of God. Biblical writers clearly did employ this view, but recent advances in theological scholarship have led growing numbers of scholars to question its validity.[25]

(v) Suffering for Others

Another biblical theory which has an especially predominant role in the New Testament, and which is extolled still by many scholars as "the most profound solution" offered by Christianity to the problem of evil, is the view that suffering contributes to the good of others. Inspired by Isaiah 40–55 (and in particular the "servant songs" contained therein), many New Testament passages espouse the view that "our suffering may be part of God's work in the world to do some greater good for other people."[26] The prime example, of course, is the redemptive suffering of Jesus, and the Christian believer supposedly can bring about good in the world by sharing in his suffering. "The 'sufferings of Christ' of the Christians," writes Schrage, "signify not only their belonging to Christ, but also the eschatological efficacy and impact of his death."[27]

This view has undeniable merit in helping people *cope* with suffering; yet it may be less successful as a means of *explaining* evil. The issue here is whether God causes evil for this or any other reason. In the case of Jesus and the early Christian community, the efficacy of this theory is clearer than it is for our present world. The suffering of Jesus was endured by him for the good of the world, and the sufferings of Paul and other early Christians were borne for the sake of spreading the Gospel amid a dangerous and hostile world. Yet, as Simundson has pointed out, it is no longer obvious that "most human suffering has a potential value for others."[28] Such a view of evil, he contends, would be troublesome to bear out in our actual experience. It is difficult, in short, for us to believe that the suffering of con-

Hyde Library
Memphis University School   30034

temporary Christians has as much to do with an explicit commitment to the faith as it did for first century Christians.

(vi) Heavenly Compensation

One of the most popular and influential means by which Christians have explained the world's suffering and evil has been to suggest that the evil will be redeemed somehow in an afterlife world. Biblical scholars inform us that this conviction became a dominant view in the apocalyptic literature and then was taken up by the New Testament writers.[29] On the day of judgment, all people supposedly will be held accountable for their words and actions: the good will be rewarded and the evil punished. Earthly suffering, it is believed, will be vindicated by God through Christ. The suffering of Jesus, in particular, is seen as an atonement and substitution for our sins: "Christ suffered once for sins, a just one for the unjust, that he might bring you to God" (1 Pet 3:18).

There is, of course, little question that the very foundation of Christian belief lies in the redemptive suffering of Jesus; yet scholarship has not reached a clear consensus as to the precise interpretation of what this means. Neither is it clear how this doctrine answers the theodicy question. Can the evil and suffering we endure in this earthly life be vindicated or "made right" in an afterlife? Indeed, is it the most viable understanding of God to view the deity as distributing rewards and punishments in a post-mortem realm? We shall see in later chapters that Hick's contemporary Irenaean theodicy insists upon the necessity of an afterlife redemption, as do most contemporary Christian theologians. This afterlife redemption, however, is understood not as compensation for evil and suffering, but rather as a fulfillment, a bringing to fruition the spiritual perfection of human beings. Process theologians, on the other hand, as we shall see also, seem to be alone (with few exceptions) in their rejection of the necessity of an afterlife domain both as an essential Christian belief and as a necessary aspect of the solution to the theodicy issue.

(vii) The Faith Solution

It is hardly surprising that several biblical passages discourage us from seeking a comprehensive solution to the problem of evil. The Bible, after all, does not present us with a uniform and complete solution, but offers many and varied answers. Thus God issues to Job out of the whirlwind the following warning: "Who is this that darkens counsel by words without knowledge?" (Job 38:2). Job soon came to acknowledge, as Paul would later proclaim, "the depth of the riches and wisdom and knowledge of God! How unsearchable are his judgments and how inscrutable his ways!" (Rom 11:33). Many biblical passages encourage us to cultivate a trusting faith in the divine plan; all evil is reconcilable with God's providential will, even though the deity's plan clearly is beyond human comprehension.

This attitude has been assessed in the previous chapter and its efficacy was questioned there; but it must be conceded that it is the faith solution (and, in particular, its exemplification in the Book of Job) which has become the standard theological response to evil. A plethora of books about the Book of Job have been written, indeed "an unmanageable mass of literature,"[30] bearing testimony to the fact that biblical writers and a large number of contemporary biblical scholars continue to find meaning in this response to the problem of evil.

Crenshaw (among other biblical scholars), however,

has argued that the faith response "represents a substantial loss of human dignity"; God's honor is saved but only at the price of "sacrificing human integrity."[31] As we have seen, the faith solution has other substantial flaws, and without a serious and introspective rational underpinning, it can lead us easily into a state of blind and passive resignation and despair.

4
Contemporary Augustinian–Thomistic Theodicy

Saint Augustine's writings on the theodicy question are recognized generally as having had more influence than those of any other Christian thinker since Saint Paul. This influence is attested to by the fact that Augustine's theodicy was utilized heavily both by Saint Thomas Aquinas and by the Protestant Reformers. It remains to this day the basis of contemporary Roman Catholic writings on theodicy and likewise continues to exert a powerful influence in conservative Protestant circles. During the past one hundred years, however, (as noted in *Chapter 1*) some scholars have begun to move beyond Augustine's all-pervasive influence.[1] John Hick's Irenaean theodicy and the theodicy proposed by process theists, among others, have led the way, and (as we shall see in the following chapters) they differ sharply from the traditional Augustinian-Thomistic theodicy at several critical points.

(i) Philosophical Themes
The Augustinian-Thomistic theodicy consists of a number of philosophical and theological themes. With respect to the former, at least four motifs are utilized in the

29

construction of the theodicy. The first is that evil has not been created by God and certainly not desired by God; evil, rather, is to be understood as the "privation of good," brought into existence by the creature. We have, in effect, deprived ourselves of potential goods by choosing evil instead of the goods which God intended for us. Charles Cardinal Journet cites and defends the relevant Augustinian text: evil is only "the privation of a good and . . . it tends to what has no existence in any way";[2] evil is not a substance or entity in its own right, but the lack of some quality or good which the thing might have had.

This theme has been elaborated by theologians and philosophers outside Catholicism as well as within. Two of the major Protestant thinkers of this century, Paul Tillich and Karl Barth, have developed an understanding of evil as "non-being," as have the influential philosophers, Martin Heidegger and Jean-Paul Sartre.[3] Yet others (John Hick, for example) have questioned the viability and usefulness of this theme. Hick points out that Augustine and Aquinas did not employ the privation theme as a solution to the problem of evil, but rather used it primarily as an argument against a dualistic solution to theodicy.[4] They wished, in other words, to emphasize that God alone is responsible for the creation of all things "out of nothing" and that any attempt to attribute evil to an evil being or beings is to be rejected. Hick condemns the philosophical account of "non-being" developed by Tillich, Barth and others, moreover, as "untenable and dangerous," as "a mistaken hypostatization of language" which is of little use in resolving the theodicy issue.[5]

A second philosophical tenet of the Augustinian-Thomistic theodicy is that which attributes evil to the "principle of plenitude." God created an extensive variety of creatures, creatures which necessarily have varying abilities and qualities, since the divine "goodness could not be adequately represented by one creature alone."[6] "The universe would not be perfect if only one grade of goodness were found in things."[7] "It pertains to divine providence that the grades of being which are possible are fulfilled" and some things will necessarily be better than others since some will have the power to fall from the good.[8] British philosopher Austin Farrer employed this principle and suggested that it implied a "mutual interference of systems":[9] the species conflict, and yet the world would be the lesser if God had chosen not to create some of the species which were possible.[10]

This theme has not gone unchallenged. Hick, among others (see, for example, also Hare and Madden[11]), has criticized its viability, suggesting that it contradicts God's voluntary creation of the world and that it leads to the despairing view, proposed by Leibniz in the eighteenth century, that this world, with its evil and pain, is the "best of all possible worlds."[12] The point here is that if this *is* in fact the best possible world, then for many people resignation and despair understandably may be the appropriate response.

A third philosophical theme used in the Augustinian-Thomistic theodicy is the so-called "aesthetic theory" of evil. This theory holds that God has created a good world, a world which *as a whole* is good; and while the individual *parts* of the world may appear to fallible human minds as evils in themselves, from God's perfect perspective, these so-called evils in fact are either *means* to good *ends* or *parts* of a good *whole*.

The Thomist philosopher Jacques Maritain, accordingly, explains that "God allows evils to happen in order to bring a greater good therefrom."[13] Yet Karl Rahner (among others) has found this view to be problematic, and has rejected its implication that suffering creatures are a necessary side-effect of an evolving world, a world which is good as a whole: "It is possible," he writes, "to imagine freedom and its dignity existing without suffering in par-adisiacal harmony," a point Journet has exploited at length.[14] The fact that freedom "has produced immense and indescribable suffering that cannot be blamed on mate-rial and biological conditions," Rahner insists, renders this explanation for evil "unsatisfactory and superficial."[15]

It is this very point, however (that God could have cre-ated a world of free creatures without evil), which itself has been challenged by many writers.[16] If God could have cre-ated a world without evil and yet a world in which creatures are free, why would an all-loving God not have exercised this option? The fact that God has not done so is a strong argument against the existence of God and undermines other aspects of the Augustinian-Thomistic theodicy, themes which imply that evil is necessary in the world.

A fourth philosophical theme employed by Thomists is the exploitation of the distinction found in the writings of Saint Thomas between God's *causing* evil and God's merely *permitting* evil. Journet, for example, has used this argument extensively, contending that since evil is not willed by God directly, the conflicts and hostility among the species are best understood as unavoidable or acciden-tal side-effects of the promotion of some great good. For God to do away with the evil side-effects would mean that God would have to do away with the species themselves.[17]

Jacques Maritain likewise has defended this point at length: God permits evil, he contends, but does not thereby cause it. Evil is "permitted by God without being in abso-lutely any way willed or caused by Him."[18] Maritain grants that God is the first cause of all things, including our free decisions; yet with respect to our evil acts, we ourselves are the first cause, with the resulting evil "known by God . . . without having been created by him."[19] Moral evil is possible where God "causes the free agent to tend to a morally good act, but which included . . . the possibility of being shattered."[20] The creature is responsible, then, in the sense that God's permissive decree does not cause the evil, but only involves the decisions not to prevent it.[21]

Austin Farrer also has defended the validity of this "double agency" concept. Farrer's analysis has been acclaimed by some recent commentators as the most careful and consistent attempt to specify what the concept actually means.[22] "Two agents for the same act," Farrer admits, "would be indeed impossible, were they both agents in the same sense and on the same level."[23] Yet, as he points out, the terms "causality" and "agency" can only be used with respect to God analogously. Farrer does admit quite candidly that the concept ultimately is beyond full human understanding, but that there are good biblical and theological arguments for its validity.[24]

Karl Rahner, interestingly enough, has challenged the traditional Thomistic distinction between God's causing and God's merely permitting evil. The distinction, he contends, is of secondary importance, since God is the sole ground and cause of all things: "Having regard to God's omnipotent freedom, which knows no bounds, causing and permitting seem to us to come so closely together that we can ask quite simply why God allows us to suffer, without having to distinguish *a priori* in this 'allowing' by God between permitting and causing."[25]

In this, Rahner shares with Luther and Calvin and many of their contemporary followers the rejection of the distinction which Aquinas and contemporary Thomists like Maritain have considered essential. Process theists, likewise, reject this double causation doctrine as a troublesome and contradictory belief (see *Chapter 6*).

(ii) Theological Themes

Besides these philosophical themes in the Augustinian-Thomistic theodicy, there are a number of important theological themes. Augustine based his theodicy largely upon the writings of Saint Paul and upon a controversial interpretation of the first three chapters of Genesis. Adam and Eve, according to Augustine's interpretation, were created perfectly, and yet they supposedly freely turned away from God and "fell" into sin. The entire human race inherited this tendency to sin, referred to by Augustine as "original sin." We are all deserving of divine punishment, accordingly, and yet God mercifully has saved some of us through the grace of Christ. All evil, according to Augustine, is the result of human sin: moral evil is caused directly by the misuse of our free will and physical evil is God's just punishment for this moral evil:[26] "An evil will is the cause of all evil," and God's "just judgment is the cause of our having to suffer from its consequences."[27]

Journet is representative among contemporary Thomists who continue to support this theodicy. "The evil of sin," he writes, "occasions the evil of punishment,"[28] although, as he explains at length, different sins (original sin, mortal sin, venial sin) call for different punishments.[29] In this teaching, Thomists are employing the Augustinian-Thomistic "principle of moral balance": God punishes sin in order to ensure the moral balance of the universe.

The conclusion drawn, then, is that human suffering is caused by human sin and also by God's just punishment of that sin. Yet the theme (considered above) that suffering is an inevitable by-product of natural laws and of conflicting species is also an essential aspect of the Thomistic theodicy. How the two themes fit together is not clear.

The basis of the Augustinian-Thomistic theodicy, nonetheless, lies in the fact that human decisions are free, despite divine providential power. This free will defense, moreover, appears to be the only explanation which has been proposed for moral evil historically and in contemporary writings; there seem to be no other possibilities. The free will explanation for evil is utilized by both Catholic and Protestant writers[30] (although Luther and Calvin rejected the authenticity of creaturely free will vis-à-vis divine causal power).[31] Augustine insisted upon the reality of free will, despite his understanding of divine omnipotence as virtually predestining all earthly decisions and events. But if we ask why God has elected some of us for blessing and some for eternal damnation, Augustine's final response is that the answer lies forever hidden from us in the mind of God.

Augustine's interpretations of the Genesis creation story and the fall of Adam and Eve, furthermore, are acknowledged by scholars as differing significantly from the original intention of the texts. Genesis, for example, does not view Adam and Eve as perfect beings in the way Augustine understands them to be,[32] nor does it say that Adam's sin was predestined by God or that Adam's progeny inherit this sin as an "original sin." Augustine's interpretation has led to several difficult theological questions: Why, for instance, would such perfect creatures sin? Indeed, is it even possible that perfect creatures could sin?

Augustine, nevertheless, argued his case persistently. Both God and human beings, for example, are said to be the cause of every act ("we may understand both that we do them, and that God makes us do them"),[33] a theme which was refined and exploited by Aquinas and which continues to be a major aspect of the contemporary Thomists' free will defense. God is the primary cause of all earthly events, and yet creatures are the secondary causes.[34] The further distinction, as noted above, regarding events being caused by God and merely permitted by God also is utilized heavily by contemporary Thomists.

Journet, for example, attributes morally evil acts to human free will and yet he holds God responsible for good human acts. "It is clear," he writes, "that the initiative" for our acts differs "according to whether the free act is good or evil." "If the free act is morally good, bringing with it positive new values, the first initiative must surely be attributed to God."[35] Sin, on the other hand, "is produced by man alone," and while it is true that God is the first cause of everything which comes about in the world, sin is not a positive being "it is a privation introduced into a positive being." Journet, accordingly, has defended the free will defense by making use of the privation theory.[36]

Maritain concurs: "God cannot be the cause of evil itself or privation, nor of the mutilation which deforms my act; of this it is I who am the first cause. Evil as such is the only thing I am able to do without God."[37] Farrer likewise defends creaturely free will and has taken a leading role in trying to delineate clearly and justify consistently how God can be understood as an agent.[38] His argument is highly complex, yet rests largely upon the concept of double agency (see above).[39] By appealing both to biblical testimony and Christian experience, Farrer claims to resolve the problem of reconciling divine predestination and human freedom by rejecting the view that God's primary causation is so all-pervasive that it renders human free will meaningless: "We know that the action of a man can be the action of God in him; our religious existence is an experimenting with this relation. Both the divine and the human actions remain real and therefore free in the union between them."[40] It is puzzling, however, that Farrer did not fully exploit his eloquent free will defense more specifically with respect to the theodicy issue.[41]

Rahner's understanding of the free will theodicy contributes an interesting and important factor. He rejects the free will argument, at least as it is interpreted as the exclusive explanation of human suffering. Such a view would set up human freedom "as somehow purely and simply absolute and underivable in its decision."[42] Our freedom is not an unconditional but rather "a created freedom, sustained in its existence and nature always and everywhere by God's supreme providence." We are indeed free, and yet our every decision is "completely embraced solely by God's disposition."[43]

In this, Rahner displays the tension within Thomism and within much of Christian thought generally: human beings are responsible for evil and yet God's omnipotent causal agency is acknowledged as the ultimate and primary cause of all things.[44] It is hardly surprising, then, that Rahner's final solution to the problem of evil is an appeal to the faith solution. He is unconvinced of the viability of any of the proposed solutions and finds meaning only in the acceptance of God in faith: "The incomprehensibility of suffering," he argues, "is part of the incomprehensibility of God." Indeed, suffering "is the form . . . in which the incomprehensibility of God himself appears."[45]

5
Contemporary Irenaean Theodicy

Since the publication of his book on theodicy, *Evil and the God of Love* (1966), John Hick has been acclaimed widely for his major contribution to the theodicy issue. Hick's utilization and systematic development of the writings of St. Irenaeus (c. 130–c. 202) has led to the construction of a theodicy which is regarded generally as the first clearly defined alternative to the Augustinian-Thomistic perspective. Hick hardly is exaggerating in suggesting that the "Augustinian picture is so familiar that it is commonly thought of as *the* Christian view of man and his sinful plight."[1] Yet, due largely to Hick's pervasive influence, it is now common practice in contemporary theological discussions of the theodicy issue to refer both to the Augustinian and Irenaean solutions as "the two major types of theodicies."

Hick's Irenaean theodicy often is referred to as a "teleological" or "developmental" theodicy; his own word for it is "soul-making" theodicy.[2] Other twentieth century proponents of this view (or who utilize major themes of this view) include the important Russian theologian Nicolas Berdyaev,[3] the American philosopher Radoslav Tsanoff,[4] British philosopher F. R. Tennant,[5] and even Farrer (whose theodicy demonstrates how the traditional Augustinian-Thomistic approach is by no means exclusive of the Irenaean).[6] The Jesuit scientist and theologian, Teilhard de Chardin, is perhaps the foremost Catholic writer to utilize this approach to theodicy.[7]

(i) Augustinian and Irenaean Theodicy

There are several significant differences between Hick's theodicy and the traditional Augustinian-Thomistic solution, the most important of which is the contrast between the belief that God created a perfect world from which human beings "fell" (Augustine's dubious interpretation of the Genesis creation account),[8] and Hick's use of the Irenaean insight that God created a world which was less than perfect (although the world *is* "perfect" in the sense that it is a "perfect" environment for the spiritual perfecting of human beings).[9] Drawing upon the distinction made by Irenaeus between the "image" and "likeness" of God (Gen 1:26),[10] Hick argues for a two-stage creation: we have been created in the image of God but not yet in God's likeness. In contemporary terminology, this refers to a first stage of creation wherein human beings developed a physical nature through a long evolutionary process, followed by a second stage wherein we presently have the opportunity and responsibility to develop our spiritual nature.

Unlike the traditional Augustinian-Thomistic theodicy, Hick's Irenaean theodicy is not centered upon the "fall" of Adam and Eve. Modern theological scholarship regards the fall as mythological rather than historical (as we have noted), and this has important implications for the theodicy issue which do not seem to have been exploited fully by traditional theodicists. Hick cautions that if we wish to continue to use the term "fall" (because of its hallowed place in Christian tradition), "we must use it to refer to the immense gap between what we actually are and what the divine intention is eventually to be" for us.[11] He then proposes a dilemma: either the fall was impossible (since it seems unlikely that perfect creatures could sin) or it was inevitable (since creatures were created imperfectly). If the former is the case, then the traditional theodicy is undercut at its root; and if the latter is the case, viable reasons must be proposed to explain why God would create imperfect creatures, knowing they would fall into sin and evil. Hick believes that his Irenaean perspective can provide such reasons.

(ii) Moral Evil

Hick argues, first of all, that God could *not* create perfect creatures which, at the same time, genuinely could be free: "In order to be a person, exercising some measure of genuine freedom, the creature must be brought into existence, not in the immediate divine presence, but at a 'distance' from God."[12] Secondly, in response to critics like Antony Flew and John Mackie, who argue that God could have created us as morally perfect and yet also as free creatures who would have used our freedom solely for good rather than evil,[13] Hick replies that "virtues which have been formed within the agent as a hard won deposit of his own right decisions in situations of challenge and temptation, are intrinsically more valuable than virtues created within him ready made and without any effort on his own part."[14] Hick concedes, in other words, that God could have created us, without logical contradiction, as wholly good and as free beings; but Hick appeals to a value judgment that this kind of creation would be of less intrinsic value than creatures which were created less perfectly but which eventually and freely formed their "perfect" moral characters.

On this point, some critics argue that Hick has conceded too much—that is, in granting that it was even possible for God to have created a world of creatures which were both free and perfect. Ninian Smart, for example, offers persuasive arguments against such a view:

> the concept *goodness* is applied to beings of a certain sort, beings who are liable to temptations, possess inclinations, have fears, tend to assert themselves and so forth; and if they were to be immunized from evil they would have to be built in a different way. But it soon becomes apparent that to rebuild them would mean that the ascription of goodness would become unintelligible, for the reasons why men are called good and bad have a connection with human nature as it is empirically discovered to be.[15]

In brief, Smart argues that the proposal that "'God might have created men wholly good' is without intelligible content."[16] Farrer, likewise, although not in this particular context, seems to concur: God, he suggests, was not content with the creation of angels as perfect beings since God wanted beings (hence, human beings) which could freely choose to love the deity.[17]

Hick's solution to the problem of moral evil, nonetheless, is that it is the result of the inevitable free choice of sinfulness by human beings who have not yet developed their full and perfect spiritual potential, the end for which God created us all. Hick believes that his free will defense is more viable than the more traditional Augustinian-Thomistic versions because his account is not founded upon the morally, scientifically and logically objectionable belief in an Adam and Eve as the perpetrators of the first human sin, a sin for which we all must suffer.[18] Neither is his account muddled with a doctrine of divine predestination nor with an understanding of divine providence which, as the primary cause of all events, ultimately, may contradict human freedom. Nor, indeed, is Hick's Irenaean perspective obliged to defend the troublesome doctrine of double predestination, the belief that God has assigned some souls to hell's fire while others are destined from eternity by God for heavenly bliss.

Hick's critics, however, are not convinced that his theodicy is successful. David Griffin, to cite one prominent example, has questioned the soundness and validity of Hick's free will defense.[19] The fact that Hick defends the classical Christian understanding of God implies that not only has his God given creatures some degree of free will but, as such, his God has the ability to revoke this freedom in order to prevent unnecessary suffering. Hick's understanding of divine power, accordingly, is such that his God could have eradicated much of the world's most gratuitous and horrific evils; yet since it does not appear to be the case that this has been done, Griffin's challenge is that "Hick must defend God's decision to allow every instance of moral evil that has occurred."[20] Hick has argued, nevertheless, that there are, in fact, good reasons why God would not take away our freedom and why God has not and does not eradicate specific evils nor evils in general (see below).

Another frequent and closely related criticism of Hick's view is that it seems absurd for an omnipotent God to "have wasted over four billion years setting the stage for the only thing thought to be intrinsically valuable, the moral and spiritual development of human beings."[21] The fact that God simply did not create the environment necessary for human growth, rather than permit so many hundreds of millions of years of seemingly unnecessary and meaningless pain, "counts against Hick's defense of the omnipotent God's total goodness."[22]

The question of animal suffering, moreover, is relevant here: Has Hick adequately accounted for such suffering? Is it sufficient to explain this profoundly devastating aspect of the world's evil merely as part of the necessary environment for human soul-making? Some of his critics find this a particularly unacceptable and offensive aspect of Hick's theodicy (see *Chapter 9* for further discussion of the issue of animal suffering and Hick's response).[23]

(iii) Physical Evil

The problem of explaining why God allows physical evil is, perhaps, an even more difficult question than the problem of moral evil. Hick's solution to this problem, as is generally the case among theodicists, is intricately related to his explanation for moral evil. For human beings to develop the spiritual natures desired by God, we must live in an environment which is appropriate for such a task. Yet, in "a world devoid both of dangers to be avoided and rewards to be won we may assume," Hick points out, "there would have been virtually no development of the human intellect and imagination" and certainly no chance for moral and spiritual growth.[24]

A number of serious critical questions have been levied against Hick's theodicy at this point,[25] and Hick has responded to many of them in the second edition (1978) of his *Evil and the God of Love* book and elsewhere.[26] It may be granted, for example, that the world was created as a person-making environment and, as such, cannot be a pain-free paradise without challenges and dangers; yet why must there be *so much evil*; and indeed, why must the distribution of evil be so *gratuitous*?[27]

Hick's response to the former question is that the amount and intensity of evil in the world is relative. Imagine, he conjectures, that God were to eliminate what we consider to be the most ghastly of evils. If, for example, cancer were eliminated, would this not make the world less hostile and speak more appropriately of God's love and care for us? Hick's point is that this suggestion leads nowhere. In a world where cancer was eliminated, "something else would rank as the worst form of natural evil" and if God were to eliminate this, then again, something else would be perceived as the worst and most gratuitous form of evil. The perception would continue "until the world was free of all natural evil"; but that would leave a world which could no longer elicit the necessary moral and spiritual growth intended by God and, hence, would defeat the whole purpose of the creation of the human species.[28]

With respect to the serious question as to why there is so much meaningless, gratuitous, undeserved suffering, Hick's response is to argue that the alternative is far more problematic. Suppose, he suggests, that good deeds were rewarded and evil deeds were punished in direct proportion to the deeds. Such a world surely would not serve a person-making purpose, for if it were evident that good was rewarded immediately and evil punished immediately, the very basis of morality would be undercut. People would act not for the sake of goodness, but out of fear of punishment for wrong acts and with expectations of rewards for good acts.[29]

(iv) Universal Salvation

A central and indispensable aspect of Hick's theodicy is his defense of the belief in an afterlife existence for all human beings, a post-mortem realm wherein all of us eventually will reach a state of spiritual perfection. The theodicy question, he insists, cannot be answered satisfactorily without this expectation. God created a world wherein creatures are less than perfect, a world wherein we human beings will fall into sin inevitably and suffer accordingly. Yet, if this world of suffering were all that God has in store for us, then Hick's point is that God would hardly be the all-loving and merciful being Christians believe the deity to be. The only conceivable justification for God's creation of imperfect creatures, Hick insists, is that we all shall be brought eventually and freely to a state of spiritual perfection. Thus, "the fulfillment of the divine purpose, as it is postulated in the Irenaean type of theodicy, presupposes each person's survival, in some form of bodily death, and further living and growing toward that end-state."[30]

Hick points out, to be sure, that heaven is not a compensation for earthly suffering, but an opportunity for continued spiritual growth. Nothing can compensate the undeserved suffering and horrors suffered by countless human beings, but the promise of an opportunity for continued spiritual growth can take away some of the sting of gratuitous suffering. Indeed, those who have suffered the most may well be the most spiritually advanced.[31]

Much controversy has centered around Hick's appeal to a heavenly fulfillment as essential to a solution to the theodicy issue. One recent commentator, Terrence Tilley, for example, expresses the familiar complaint that Hick's expectation of universal salvation "seeks to explain the present obscurity {why God permits evil} by an appeal to a future even more obscure."[32] Hick's appeal to a heaven demonstrates at best, in other words, that there *might* be an explanation in the future, but this hope hardly provides an explanation for present evils. This criticism, we might add, applies to the countless number of writers, contemporary and historical, who posit a heavenly justification for present evils: such a belief does not explain the world's evils, but merely postpones the solution to the supernatural and purely speculative dimension.[33]

Another frequent and closely related criticism of Hick's eschatological hope is, as Stephen Davis has argued, that there seems to be "no convincing evidence that the human race is improving morally or spiritually."[34] Indeed, as Davis asks, is this life really of any value to God or to ourselves, since most (all?) human beings die long before reaching spiritual perfection? Indeed, if we are to continue on our journey toward this goal in the afterlife, does this not undermine profoundly the value and meaning of our present lives?

Whether or not a "universal salvation" is consistent with Christian belief and doctrine is another interesting problem Hick has been called upon to defend.[35] He has been challenged also to explain how universal salvation is not inconsistent with (i. e., contradictory to) human free will.[36]

Hick, of course, is aware of these criticisms and has responded in various places. The debate continues, and while his Irenaean theodicy certainly has offered fresh and important insights into the theodicy issue, it also contains, obviously, a new set of problems.

6
Process Theodicy

The writings of the process philosophers Alfred North Whitehead and Charles Hartshorne have made a significant impact upon contemporary philosophical and theological thought. Whitehead's important insights concerning the nature of God and Hartshorne's call for a serious "new look at the problem of evil,"[1] together with the writings of other process theists like David Griffin,[2] have contributed much to the contemporary discussions on the theodicy issue.

Process theists insist that the historical formulation of the theodicy problem can be "dissolved."[3] The traditional discussion has been, in Hartshorne's opinion, a mistake, a "pseudoproblem,"[4] perpetrated by "a mass of undigested notions too vague or self-inconsistent to permit any useful application of rational argument."[5] His main complaint is that the manner in which the theodicy question has been posed is problematic and, as such, insures that the conventional answers themselves are problematic. In short, traditional theists have had a confused and untenable belief about the meaning and definition of the term "God" and also about what it means to be a creature. "'God,' it was held, was a being perfect in every way, and hence in power and goodness. It was supposed, accordingly, that a being perfect in power must have the power to prevent anything undesirable from occurring."[6] The fact that God has not done so has led to the variety of familiar explanations for the devastating presence of evil and suffering in the world, proposals which range from the divine punishment explanation, to redemptive suffering with Christ, as we have seen.

Process writers reject what they understand to be the well-established interpretation of divine power (and also the interpretations of many of the other divine attributes, as they have been conceived traditionally).[7] The conventional Thomistic distinction, for example, between God as primary cause and creatures as secondary causes is rejected by Hartshorne as misleading and meaningless "verbiage."[8] God certainly is intimately involved in creaturely life, a point which process theists take great pains to explain, but not in the conventional sense (as it is interpreted by process thinkers) which apparently gives to God a deterministic monopoly of power.

Griffin has written a detailed critique of the traditional, Christian understanding of God as it is represented in such seminal figures as Augustine, Aquinas, Luther, Calvin, Barth, and others,[9] a critique which exploits and expands upon Whitehead's warning that traditional theology has passed over "the Galilean origin of Christianity" which revealed a God who "dwells upon the tender elements of the world, [and who] which slowly and in quietness operates by love."[10] In its place, Christianity accepted a tyrant, a dictator, a God who "omnipotently disposes a wholly derivative world."[11] Process writers distinguish between (what they perceive to be) the God of *coercive* power in traditional theism and a God who acts solely *persuasively*, the latter being a far more viable belief.[12]

Process writers are aware that their conception of God

has been criticized consistently as being too limited, too weak, and hence, as unworthy of worship. One of the earliest of these critics was Stephen Ely,[13] and this particular criticism has been repeated endlessly in the writings of numerous commentators for many decades. Hick, for example, states that "the fundamental criticism of a process theodicy must be a criticism of the doctrine of a limited God."[14] Sontag agrees, and accuses process theists of returning to the contentious Platonic concept of a limited deity.[15] Davis likewise rejects the process God as a "denial of the traditional Christian view of omnipotence."[16] A solely persuasive God, he insists, is too weak to merit the appellation of deity.[17]

Process theists are resolute, nevertheless, in defending the religious viability of their understanding of God. Hartshorne, for example, has argued that if God *were* omnipotent (in the sense which he and other process theists understand to be implied in the traditional formulation), then God literally would have "all the power" and creatures would have no power whatsoever. But, of course, if God's power were exerted over creatures with no power, the term "omnipotence" would be meaningless. Indeed, further, even if God voluntarily has given some power to creatures, as the traditional theology holds, that power (in theory at least) can be revoked at any time. As such, God must take full responsibility for the evil and suffering in the world, since creaturely freedom, apparently, has not been rescinded from time to time.

Griffin challenges Hick on this point, arguing that the traditional God espoused by Hick (despite his radically non-traditional theodicy) "could have found some happier middle ground between our present, all-too-destructive world, and the 'hedonistic paradise' Hick fears would make us morally and spiritually flabby."[18] Hartshorne, moreover, insists that we pay unnecessary "metaphysical compli-ments" to God in attributing to the deity impossible and meaningless attributes. Process thinkers are convinced that their revised conception of deity is far more coherent than the traditional interpretation, and that their vision of God is the basis for a much more meaningful solution to the theodicy problem.

There have been protests, nevertheless, against the use which process theists make of the terms "persuasion" and "coercion" as they apply to divine causal power. Process writers have not been clear enough as to the precise mean-ings of these terms, an issue which has become a matter of contention both outside and within process circles.[19] At the same time, the common practice among many process theists of describing the traditional God as acting solely coercively may well be as inaccurate an interpretation as it is offensive and unacceptable to traditional theists.[20]

(i) Free Will and Evil

Process theists reject both the conventional use of the free will defense (since the traditional doctrine of God seems to negate free will among creatures) and other ver-sions, like that of John Hick, whose type of argument seems to make God ultimately responsible for evil by not interceding from time to time, despite having the power to do so. Yet process theists defend a revised version of the free will solution, a defense supported by a novel under-standing of God's causal interaction with creatures.

The argument is that all creatures are sentient, to vary-ing degrees at least, depending upon their level of mental sophistication. Whitehead's metaphysical scheme argues that all reality is constituted by "actual entities" or "exper-ient-occasions,"[21] groupings of which form the objects of our sense perception. All creatures (i. e., the myriad of actual entities which constitute all creatures) are in the continual process of synthesizing the data of the environment into new experiences, into new concrete actualizations of what had been merely indeterminate potentiality.

All creatures, moreover, not only are sentient and display some degree of creativity, but on the human level this creativity has evolved into a conscious freedom. The argument of process theists here is against any form of determinism, whether it be a causal determinism by the world, by our own characters, or by God. Human beings are free in the sense that the causal antecedents of every new experience limit the possibilities of the experience but are never the "necessary and sufficient causes" of the new experiences.[22]

God's role is not to determine our decisions nor to interfere with natural laws, but to provide what Whitehead referred to as the "initial subjective aim" for each experience. The "divine method of world control is called 'persuasion' by Whitehead," in comparison with the traditional view which attributes to God "all the power there is."[23] The argument is for a "division of powers," for a mutual influence between God and creatures.[24]

This, according to Hartshorne, is "the minimal solution" to the problem of evil.[25] "Risk of evil and opportunity for good are two aspects of just one thing: multiple freedom. . . . This is the sole, but sufficient, reason for evil as such and in general."[26]

(ii) Physical Evil

The problem of explaining physical evil is typically a far more difficult one than the problem of explaining moral evil, as we have pointed out. Process theists, however, see the two solutions as one, more or less, since a line cannot be drawn between sentient and supposedly lifeless aspects of reality. All entities have at least some degree of creativity and in non-human entities physical evils result from the interaction of this creativity. Hartshorne argues, accordingly, that with "a multiplicity of creative agents, some risk of conflict and suffering is inevitable."[27] God has determined the limits of creaturely power and while the deity could have determined these limits otherwise than is the case, God cannot eliminate the creativity itself: to be a creature is by definition to be creative.[28] God's role "is not to enforce a maximal ratio of good to evil, but a maximal ratio of chances of good to chances of evil."[29]

For process writers, God did not create the world *ex nihilo*, but rather created the known universe out of some pre-existent actualities. This interpretation certainly is not consistent with traditional Christian belief, as many critics have pointed out,[30] but process theists defend its theological viability on several grounds, insisting (for example) that it is consistent with the biblical creation accounts.[31]

Process theists argue, moreover, that if God in fact had created the world "out of nothing," then human beings (and all other levels of creatures) would be dependent absolutely upon God. As such, our freedom would not then be inherent, but would have been given by God, and this would imply that our freedom could be overridden by God at any time. The fact that so much evil has arisen from our free acts and that these acts have *not* been overridden by God, accordingly, makes the deity responsible for this apparently avoidable evil and misery.[32] Griffin makes the point here that God, as traditionally conceived (as the all-powerful creator "out of nothing"), presumably could have eliminated certain evils without in any way seriously affecting creaturely freedom.[33]

Griffin has proposed an alternative view—namely,

that there are some eternal, uncreated, necessary principles about the way actualities can be ordered and which limit the sorts of situations which are possible. This implies that there is in the creature a fundamental, innate creativity, a view which has been criticized, to be sure, as denying the all-powerfulness of God. Yet process theists, as we have noted above, have significant counter-arguments in support of their understanding of divine power. Many critics of the process view seem to hold, mistakenly, that process theists espouse the position that there are entities which exist not just eternally but independently of God; this certainly would lead to an unacceptable form of dualism. But in my study of Hartshorne's theodicy, *Evil and the Process God*, I have tried to show that this "other" which exists eternally (even if it be a mere chaos) is now and always has and will be totally dependent for its existence upon God. The "other," in effect, is immanent in God, and always has been.[34]

This position is called "panentheism," and is proposed by process theists in contradistinction to both traditional theism (which sees an absolute separation between God and the world) and pantheism (which simply identifies God and the world). Process theists argue that God is the whole of reality, while the world is merely a part of God, a modest part of the infinite potential within the reality of God, the potential which has been actualized. There persists in God a boundless abyss of creative potential which remains unactualized.[35] The main point here of the process theists is the concern to defend the conviction that divine causal action cannot fully determine the creature, for to be a creature is, by definition, to be not only creative but dependent upon God, *sine qua non* ("without which not"; i. e., without which nothing could exist).

(iii) Aesthetic Value

An essential feature of the process theodicy is the argument that our capacity for self-determination and for influencing others has evolved in direct proportion to our capacity to experience ever-greater goods and to suffer ever-greater evils.[36] Before we evolved into human beings, both the good we could experience and our potential for evil and suffering were far less than they now are. In contrast to Hick's theory that God created us in a harsh world so that we would have the proper environment for soul-making, the process argument is that the reason for the divine luring of the chaos into ever-more sophisticated creatures was to avoid the evil of triviality: had the primeval chaos been left a primitive chaos fifteen billion years ago, an incredible amount of value would have been left unactualized, and this would have been a great evil in itself.[37]

Process writers argue that it is mistaken to think that an orderly utopia, one in which no evil and suffering would exist, is consistent with belief in an omnibenevolent and all-powerful God. God's purpose for us is to provide us with, and lure us toward, experiences which avoid the extremes of absolute order (regularity, predictability), on the one hand, and superficiality (trivial experiences), on the other hand. For each level of being, "there is a balance of unity and diversity," writes Hartshorne, "which is ideally satisfying."[38] All levels of creatures experience value; that is, all creatures have experiences which have a potentially appropriate degree of both variety and intensity. "God's purpose in the creative advance is the evocation of intensities."[39]

This understanding of the aesthetic value in all of our experiences has the effect of softening somewhat the harsh reality of evil. Evil is real and devastating, and yet there is some minimal value in every experience, value we can appropriate if we follow God's lure toward its actualization. Process theists soften the reality of evil also by insisting, in agreement with growing numbers of contemporary writers, that *God suffers* along with us. God is, as Whitehead put it in a now famous phrase, "the fellow sufferer who understands."[40] Griffin's comment on this point is that the God who suffers with us is the one being who is in the position to know whether the goods we have achieved are worth the price of the evils we have had to endure, an issue frequently raised by critics. The fact that God has lured the chaos into a continually more complex world somewhat assures us, Griffin notes, that it all indeed *is* worthwhile and valuable.[41]

There are, of course, critics of this significant reliance by process theists upon the aesthetic dimension of value. The main argument is that process theists invalidly place aesthetic concerns over ethical ones. Hare and Madden, for example, contend that "a God who is willing to pay any amount in moral and physical evil to gain aesthetic value is an unlovable being."[42] The process God, they contend, "sacrifices human feelings to aesthetic ends."[43] Hick concurs: the process God, in his view, is the God of the "elite," the God of "the great and successful among mankind," but not the God of the countless millions who suffer wasted lives.[44] Hick's point is that the aesthetic criterion of value in process thought wrongly justifies all the evil and misery in the world as necessary by-products of the great goods which have evolved: "the good that has occurred {supposedly} renders worthwhile all the wickedness that has been committed and all the suffering that has been endured."[45]

(iv) Evil Overcome by God

Hick and much of traditional thinking about the problem of evil, as we have seen, argue that an afterlife redemption is an essential and indispensable aspect of the solution to the theodicy issue. Process thinkers, however, repudiate this argument. Rather than speculating that human beings will "live on" in some post-mortem world and that we shall reach a state of perfection and fullness, process theists argue that our immortality is "objective," rather than "subjective."[46] By this they mean that we shall survive only as objects in God's eternal reality, but not as conscious subjects. There is no afterlife reward or punishment, nor will there be any endless opportunities for compensation or fulfillment.

Many critics of process thought find this point particularly inappropriate, for it appears to contradict the very essence of Christian belief. Process thought, in other words, lacking the doctrine of a conscious immortality, seems to be without an eschatology, an eschatology which supposedly is indispensable for Christianity.[47] Yet process thinkers have attempted to counter this fundamental problem by arguing that the crucial question is *not* whether human life continues in a conscious state after death, but whether human life has any ultimate meaning and value eternally and, indeed, here and now. The aesthetic nature of life assures process theists that there is value in every earthly experience, no matter how bleak many of these experiences may be. Our purpose is to experience as much value as we have the opportunity to experience in this life; to ask or expect that we shall live on eternally and experience ever new values endlessly is, in the minds of process thinkers, tantamount to asking that we be other than we are, indeed that we become God-like, for God alone is capable of achieving endless value.

We have been created by God as finite creatures, process theists hold, and we must realize that it is God who alone is eternal. We have the opportunity, however, to *live* eternally in God. All that we have experienced and accomplished in our lives, good and evil, is immortal in this sense. Theodicy does not require that we have the chance to be perfected in a post-mortem existence. This, to be sure, is a very contentious issue and one which is far from being settled. There are, in fact, many process writers who themselves seek and argue *for* a doctrine of conscious immortality, despite Whitehead's ambiguity on the question and Hartshorne's forceful arguments against its probability.[48]

7
Philosophical Theodicies

In the preceding chapters, we have discussed some of the most prominent and important of the contemporary writings on the theodicy issue. There are, however, various other writers and positions which most assuredly merit our attention. The sheer volume of material and the complexity of the topic precludes, unfortunately, a discussion of many of these relevant writings. Yet, in this and in the following chapter, we shall consider some of the most prominent and influential of these contributions. This chapter will discuss a number of the more *philosophically* oriented theodicies: Schlesinger's proposed solution to the question; Plantinga's free will defense; Mackie and Flew on divine omnipotence and free will; and the theodicies of natural evil constructed by Swinburne and Reichenbach. The following chapter will consider some of the more *conservative* and popular of the contemporary approaches.

(i) Schlesinger's Greatest Happiness Solution

George Schlesinger is one of the few contemporary writers who has been willing to make the startling claim that the problem of evil can be resolved.[1] Not many theologians and philosophers would accept this claim,[2] although there certainly are some who have hailed Schlesinger's theodicy as "ingenious," "original" and "novel," indeed, as "the most significant contribution to the problem of theodicy since Leibniz."[3] His arguments undeniably are important and certainly are intriguing.

Schlesinger argues that while it might seem reasonable to think that an omnibenevolent, omniscient and omnipotent God would have created the best of all possible worlds, this expectation is, in fact, quite unrealistic. One of the main tenets of his argument is to point out that "divine goodness is entirely different in kind from human goodness and, consequently, should not be judged in terms of notions formed on the basis of our acquaintance with the latter."[4] Thus, while it may be morally reprehensible for *human beings* "not to do as much as one *possibly* can to make others happy," this demand logically cannot apply to *God*.[5] God cannot produce a greatest state of happiness for us any more than God can create the greatest integer. Both are logical impossibilities.[6]

Schlesinger's point is that since "there is no *prima facie* case for saying that the greatest possibilities for happiness are finite, God's inability to create the greatest state of happiness" cannot be used as evidence against the existence of the deity.[7] If God had created a world with far less evil, a world with much happier people, the problem of evil still would remain: creatures could conceive an endless list of requirements, the fulfillment of which would increase their happiness even further. If God had diminished the amount of suffering, moreover, until it vanished completely, the problem of evil would not be resolved: God would have a world of happy creatures, but since God would be aware of even greater possibilities for happiness which creatures could have had, this would render the deity morally reprehensible. The amount of evil in the world, consequently, in Schlesinger's view, is "entirely irrelevant and cannot be introduced as evidence concerning the moral nature of God."[8]

This solution to the theodicy problem has been criticized by a number of writers. Jay Rosenberg, for example, contends that while Schlesinger is correct in holding that we cannot state what kind of world God should have created, we can stipulate, nevertheless, what type of world a deity ought *not* to have created.[9] God, he insists, should not have created a world in which the actual degree of happiness falls short of the potential degree.[10]

Winslow Shea elaborates upon this critique, contending that (despite Schlesinger's arguments) a greatest possible happiness *is* logically possible. His somewhat complex argument concludes that while it is possible that the series of possible states of happiness is *finite*, it may well be *infinite*, nevertheless, yet with an upper and a lower limit. The point he makes is that "in either case a greatest happiness is logically possible, and therefore an omnipotent being could have, and possibly should have, created it."[11]

Shea maintains also that, even if one were to grant the viability of Schlesinger's argument, the consequences would be problematic: Schlesinger's God is unworthy of worship: "If He cannot be blamed for not creating more happiness than He did create, on the ground that otherwise no matter how much happiness He created He could still be blamed for not creating more of it, then it seems to me," Shea writes, that God "cannot be praised for having created any happiness at all."[12] He concludes that Schlesinger's God is infinitely inferior to what deity might have been since "the deity has created a world infinitely worse than millions of worlds He could have made."[13]

(ii) Plantinga's Free Will Defense

The free will defense has been a prominent feature of theodicy since at least the time of Saint Augustine. There are many contemporary advocates of this defense, the most influential of whom generally is considered to be Alvin Plantinga.[14]

Plantinga distinguishes his use of the free will *defense* from a free will *theodicy* (like that found in Saint Augustine, for example, and in numerous other writers). A free will theodicy is an attempt to explain why there is evil in the world, while Plantinga's defense is the more modest attempt to show merely (yet significantly) that evil is not incoherent with belief in God.

Plantinga denies the arguments put forth by contemporary philosophers like Mackie and Flew, arguments which insist that God "could have created significantly free creatures" and yet have caused them "to always do only what's right."[15] Plantinga is aware that many philosophers endorse a "compatibilist" analysis of freedom, according to which it is assumed to be possible that some actions are free, despite the fact that they are all causally determined by events entirely outside our control.[16] Plantinga's point, however, is that if this were true, the free will defense would fail; he has offered detailed and complex arguments against its being true.

A major premise of the free will defense is that it is possible that God considers it more valuable that there be moral goods, goods which result from the moral activity of creatures freely doing what is right (and also the concurrent possibility of suffering and evil), than to have a universe without such goods and evils.[17] Plantinga concedes that there may be many possible worlds which display a better balance of good and evil than does our actual world, worlds which may be populated with significantly free creatures who do only what is right. Yet his point is that it is *possible* that it was not within the power of God to actualize any of them, despite the fact that God is omnipotent.[18] He has defended this claim by arguing that it is logically impossible for God to *cause* free actions in creatures.[19]

Plantinga's writings on the free will defense have given rise to an impressive array of commentaries, both supportive and critical. His writings are highly complex and he not only has exploited his considerable technical skills as a logician, but also has made ample use of logical symbolism to formalize his argumentation. Unfortunately, many of the attacks upon his position have missed his basic point that he has attempted to construct a defense, not a theodicy.[20]

Hick, for example, argues against Plantinga's claim that the amount of evil in the world does not render the existence of God unlikely or improbable.[21] Hick charges Plantinga, accordingly, with failing to deal with the "substantial problem";[22] he finds fault, in other words, with Plantinga's lack of a theodicy. Yet, besides the fact that this type of criticism has missed Plantinga's point, the latter's recent work in probability theory seems, nevertheless, to answer criticisms like Hick's. Plantinga has, in short, attempted to show that it simply is not true that the amount of evil in the world renders God's existence improbable or unlikely.[23]

Another problem which is often cited, however, focuses upon Plantinga's appeal to the devil as the cause of physical evils: a host of critics find this extremely naive and implausible in our enlightened day and age.[24] Plantinga, nonetheless, has defended his appeal to Satan (although rather weakly) by arguing, essentially, that Christians who believe in a supernatural being called "God" should not find it implausible to believe also in a supernatural evil power.[25] A better approach, perhaps, has been argued by David Basinger, for example, who has sought to demonstrate that Plantinga's free will defense actually does not need the controversial appeal to Satan. It must only be shown that just as God cannot unilaterally bring it about that free creatures always act for good ends, so neither can God unilaterally bring it about that "events in nature be perfectly correlated to the needs of specific humans."[26]

Plantinga's understanding, finally, of divine omnipotence has been questioned by many commentators. Pike, for example, has argued that the concept can be defended only if it can be shown that God has the ability to use the world's evils for an ultimately good end.[27] Plantinga's delimitation of the theodicy issue to a defense rather than a solution which would have incorporated some appeal to the mystery of divine salvation (the aspect Pike finds lacking) renders his theodicy "theologically incomplete." Indeed, as commentator Kenneth Surin has argued, "the very simplicity of Plantinga's proposal for resolving the 'problem of evil' is ... problematic. His beguiling 'minimalism' {leads to} ... a pared down theodicy acceptable to the theodicist with greatly reduced or even no real *theological* expectations."[28]

(iii) Mackie and Flew on Free Will and Omnipotence

Plantinga's argument that it is logically impossible for God to create creatures such that they always freely perform good actions has been recognized as one way to answer the well-known criticism of John Mackie and Antony Flew against the viability of the free will defense.[29] Their challenge has been to insist that if God *really* were omnipotent, God could have created a world in which free beings *always* freely choose what is good. Mackie's main contention is that God was not faced with the choice between creating free beings which inevitably would use their freedom for evil as well as for good, on the one hand, and creating innocent automata with no freedom, automata which would be conditioned to do only good, on the other hand. There "was open to {God} the obviously better possibility of making beings who would act freely but always go right." That God did not do so "is inconsistent" with being both omnipotent and wholly good" and this "is sufficient to dispose of" the free will solution.[30]

Flew's argument makes a similar point: since a free action is one which is not externally compelled but one which flows from the nature of the agent, such action is not incompatible with its being caused: God could have, without contradiction, "created people who would always as a matter of fact freely have chosen to do the right thing."[31]

In his free will defense, Plantinga has attempted to answer this notable charge of Flew and Mackie,[32] as he does also in his appeal (not mentioned in the previous discussion) to a "transworld depravity." It is possible, he argues, that every human being is depraved to the extent that everyone will freely choose wrongly on at least one occasion.[33] If this is the case, then it is *possible* that God could not have created free creatures who always choose good.

(iii) Swinburne and Reichenbach:
Theodicies of Natural Evil

The free will defense attempts to show that the existence of moral evil is not logically incompatible with God's existence. Whether it has been defended satisfactorily is a contentious point, yet, in any event, the problem of natural or physical evil remains: how are such evils as disease, birth defects, droughts, famines, and so on, to be reconciled with the existence of an all-powerful and all-loving God? The traditional Augustinian theodicy, which attributes natural evil to divine punishment or to divinely orchestrated tests of faith, and so on (as we have seen), is less than adequate in the minds of many contemporary writers, as is Plantinga's appeal to evil powers as the cause of natural evils. The Thomist view of natural evil as an inevitable by-product of natural laws which are necessary for human life may be more tenable as an explanation, as is the view of John Hick that natural evils serve as the necessary environment for human "soul-making."

Yet Richard Swinburne's theodicy of natural evils has gained widespread attention among contemporary scholars.[34] His view offers fresh insights into this question, and (while controversial)[35] at the very least his theodicy supplements what is best in the aforementioned solutions to the problem of natural evil. Bruce Reichenbach also has done much work recently on this problem, and we shall refer to his writings briefly after a discussion of Swinburne's work.[36]

Swinburne sees natural evil as a necessary condition for human free will. Natural evils, he explains, "are necessary if agents are to have the *knowledge* of how to bring about evil or prevent its occurrence, knowledge which they must have if they are to have a genuine choice between bringing about evil and bringing about good."[37] Swinburne explains that we acquire knowledge of the consequences of our actions from the consequences of past actions. We come to know that certain actions have harmful effects through the cumulative experience of such injurious consequences. "There must be naturally occurring evils," he concludes, "if men are to know how to cause evils themselves or are to prevent evil occurring. And there have to be *many* such evils, if men are to have sure knowledge,"[38] knowledge which is induced from past experiences.

The "crux of the problem of evil,"[39] however, as Swinburne and most others recognize, is the *quantity* of evil in

the world. This objection is a serious obstacle to belief in
the existence of God: *some* evil is necessary if we are to be
free agents, yet the question is whether God has "inflicted
too much suffering on too many people (and animals) to
give knowledge to others for the sake of the freedom of the
latter."[40] Swinburne's response is that there are divinely
imposed limits to the amount of suffering given to us. Just
as there is a temporal limit, for example, (since we all must
die) so must there be, presumably, a limit to the intensity
and depth of possible suffering set by the constitution of the
brain.

Critics still insist, nevertheless, that the limit is too
wide, that we suffer far too much to justify the good which
may result. To this concern, Swinburne has responded:

> the trouble is that the fewer natural evils a God pro-
> vides, the less opportunity he provides for man to exer-
> cise responsibility. For the less natural evil, the less
> knowledge he gives to man of how to produce or avoid
> suffering and disaster, the less opportunity for his exer-
> cise of the higher virtues, and the less experience of the
> harsh possibilities of existence; and the less he allows
> to men the opportunity to bring about large-scale hor-
> rors, the less the freedom and responsibility which he
> gives to them.

The alternative would have been for God to have created
"a toy-world, a world where things matter, but not very
much; where we can choose and our choices can make a
small difference, but the real choices remain God's. For he
simply would not allow us the choice of doing real harm."[41]

Commentators on Swinburne's theodicy have raised
several other issues. Surin questions, for example, the justice of Swinburne's God: how can a just God allow countless millions of innocent people to suffer (Hiroshima, the

Black Death, etc.) for the sake of others to learn to act responsibly?[42] Eleonore Stump, furthermore, queries whether it is necessary, for instance, that knowledge of the consequences of our actions must come from induction on the basis of past experience. Why cannot God provide this knowledge directly (not "face to face," a possibility which Swinburne rejects, but perhaps) in a series of vivid, message-laden dreams which could be verified by subsequent scientific testing?[43] This knowledge, in some cases at least, could also be gained by scientific means, Stump suggests, rather than through supernaturally induced means.

David Acinar, moreover, argues for the validity of the verbal knowledge God could give us "face to face," despite Swinburne's rejection of this possibility. God, he proposes, could implant the needed data in our brains prior to birth so that the relevant information would come to consciousness when it is needed in various life circumstances, thereby eliminating the need for so much natural evil.[44]

But let us turn now to Reichenbach's theodicy of natural evil. It is not as well known nor as controversial as Swinburne's, yet it certainly deserves mention, if only briefly. Where Swinburne argues that natural evils are necessary for there to be a meaningful human freedom, Reichenbach's more modest claim is that the possibility of natural evil is inherent in the system of natural laws which supports human life. He rejects, then, the claim of numerous atheistic (or at least skeptical) critics that natural evil is more than sufficient ground for rejecting belief in God.

McCloskey, for example, has argued that if God really existed, God could eliminate natural evils by miraculous intervention or by having created a very different world in the first place.[45] Reichenbach's response has been to point out that divine intervention is a dangerous concept which would, if in fact it did occur, destabilize the world to the extent that rationality itself would be in jeopardy. In such a world, "there would be no necessary relation between phenomena, and in particular between cause and effect."[46] In such a world, "agents could not entertain rational expectations, make predictions, estimate probabilities, or calculate prudence. They would not be able to know what to expect about any course of action they would like to take. Whether or not such action would be possible . . . would be unknown or unknowable."[47]

Reichenbach contends, in short, that a world which functioned by intermittent divine intervention (miracles) would be a world which is incompatible with the existence of genuinely free and moral agents. This simply was not a viable option, accordingly, for God to actualize, since divine interventions would imply that "agents could not will evil, and even if they could, the evil which they willed could not be actualized," since God would permit no evil to occur.[48]

With respect to McCloskey's second point, that God could have created a world with different natural laws in order to prevent or eliminate natural evils, Reichenbach's response is to argue that this criticism also is flawed, "for to introduce different natural laws would entail alteration of the objects governed by those laws."[49] He appeals to F. R. Tennant who made this point most precisely:

> To illustrate what is here meant: if water is to have the various properties in virtue of which it plays its beneficial part in the economy of the physical world and the life of mankind, it cannot at the same time lack its obnoxious capacity to drown us. The specific gravity of water is as much a necessary outcome of its ultimate constitution as its freezing point, or its thirst-quenching and cleansing functions. There cannot be assigned

to any substance an arbitrarily selected group of qualities, from which all that ever may prove unfortunate to
any sentient organism can be eliminated, especially if
. . . the world . . . is to be a calculable cosmos.[50]

The point is the same for human beings as it is for natural entities like water: God cannot create a different set of
natural laws without affecting the nature of water, nor can
God do so without altering the very constitution of human
beings themselves.[51]

8
Conservative and Popular Theodicies

In this chapter, we continue the discussion of a number of other significant perspectives on the theodicy issue, writings which have been influential especially among non-professional theologians and which are of a far more traditional flavor than those discussed in the previous three chapters. We shall consider the highly influential writings of C. S. Lewis; the theodicy of conservative evangelical theologians; and Rabbi Kushner's best-selling book which has popularized and dramatically contributed to a general interest in the theodicy issue. The chapter concludes with a discussion of the question of divine power and divine suffering. This latter issue certainly is not to be considered traditional or conservative thinking, but it is an appropriate conclusion to this chapter since the theme of divine power and suffering emanates directly, as we shall see, from the issues discussed in the preceding sections of the chapter.

(i) C. S. Lewis and Conservative Theodicy
C. S. Lewis has proposed a theodicy which is far more conservative (i.e., traditional) than the theodicies discussed in the previous three chapters. His perspective has much in

common with the Augustinian tradition (see *Chapter 4*), yet the fact that his writings have had an extraordinary influence upon Christian laypeople justifies giving them independent consideration here.[1]

Lewis' writings have been criticized as a "vulgar" popularization of fundamentalism, whose "literalism" and "complete ignorance" of modern biblical scholarship is not only "shocking" but "intellectually subversive."[2] Yet, Lewis has a host of supporters who have produced a steady stream of literature about him, most of which has lacked serious critical assessment, preferring instead to elevate him to a figure of almost cult status.[3]

His theodicy most assuredly is conservative in the sense that he considers not only that the evil and suffering in the world is the result of fallen angels, but that pain is the instrument which God implements to rescue us from our fallen state and inadequate faith in order to bring us to a much more profound faith. As one recent commentator puts it, "God's task," for Lewis, "is not only to accept us but to make us acceptable to him. To experience pain forces humanity into a more loving shape—less egoistic, less rebellious, more willing to be loved by someone outside of themselves."[4] If we reject pain's remedial influence, we reject God and our heavenly hope, choosing instead eternal separation from God. Pain is "God's megaphone,"[5] then, whereby our rebellious nature and illusory vision of the world is broken.

For Lewis, the fact that the world is filled with pain does not contradict *divine benevolence*. He argued that just the opposite is the case: pain is evidence of God's loving care for us. Pain is the only means to salvation. Neither, indeed, is *divine omnipotence* threatened by the preponderance of evil and suffering in the world: Lewis contends that it was logically impossible for God to have created both free creatures and a world without a fixed structure. Our misuse of free will causes most of the world's evil; the rest is caused by the necessity of natural laws which support human life. He explains this as follows:

> We can, perhaps, conceive of a world in which God corrected the results of this abuse of free will by His creatures at every moment; so that a wooden beam became soft as grass when it was used as a weapon, and the air refused to obey me if I attempted to set up in it the sound waves that carry lies or insults. But such a world would be one in which wrong actions were impossible, and in which, therefore, freedom of the will would be void.[6]

Lewis, of course, did not argue that *all* of the pain we suffer is given to us by God deliberately in order to restore us to a healthy spiritual state. We have genuine free will and we ourselves cause most of the world's evil, the moral evil, certainly. Nature's fixed laws, to be sure, account for the numerous forms of natural evil, and yet Lewis' main point was to underscore the fact that we are fallen and depraved creatures which, as such, have an indisputable propensity toward sin. We need to open ourselves to divine grace to be restored to spiritual health.

Lewis was aware that there is considerable theological controversy about the extent to which we human beings contribute freely to our actions, on the one hand, and how much God controls, on the other hand. He pointed out correctly that the Bible speaks both of free will ("Work out your salvation in fear and trembling") and divine causation ("for it is God who works in you"). Yet whether Lewis has responded adequately to this profound and infamous issue clearly is a serious problem. His position is close to the conservative Christianity which attributes all goods and all evils to God—despite the fact that he has offered alternative reasons for good and evil via his free will account and the natural law argument.

Lewis' well-known writings on miracles confirm this point:[7] God has the power, he insists, to intervene occasionally in the normal course of natural events. This is most certainly a very controversial point, yet Lewis believed that there were no convincing arguments against the possibility of such intermittent miracles.[8]

Conservative evangelical theology has emphasized divine determinism far more unequivocally. This dimension of Christianity is not far removed from the traditional, Augustinian tradition, yet (as was the case with C. S. Lewis) it merits independent discussion here because of its immense popularity. One of its major proponents, Carl Henry, has argued that on the basis of scripture and experience, "all history reveals the certainty of events decreed by God."[9] Arthur Pink, moreover, defines divine sovereignty as implying that God has "all power in heaven and earth, so that none can defeat his council, thwart his purpose, or resist his will."[10] August Strong,[11] Andrew Rule,[12] J. I. Packer,[13] and a host of other evangelical writers agree: God is responsible for the good and evil in the world. Yet the common conservative view is not only that "God is sovereign," but also that "we are responsible."[14]

There are, interestingly, a minority of evangelical writers who have begun to question this age-old and rather troublesome view. John Claypool, Richard Foster, Anthony Campolo, among others,[15] for example, have been reconsidering the paradox of divine power in its relationship to human freedom. The compromise most often suggested by such writers is that God's power has been self-limited to permit meaningful human freedom, a view consistent with Hick and many other non-evangelical Christian theologians.

(ii) Kushner's Popularization of Theodicy

Rabbi Kushner's book, *When Bad Things Happen to Good People*,[16] has had an enormous influence upon lay-people since its publication in 1981. It is a non-technical book, written by a religious man whose child died after a terrible ten year ordeal with a terminal illness. The theodicy question, aptly reflected in the title of Kushner's book, is the "only question which really matters: why do bad things happen to good people?"[17] "Can I," Kushner queries, "continue to teach people that the world is good, and that a kind and loving God is responsible for what happens in it," when we are assaulted daily with tragedies: senseless murders, young people killed in automobile accidents, and an endless list of other incredibly horrible and demoralizing calamities?

Kushner rejects the more traditional views which have been proposed to explain suffering; in particular, he questions the predominant view that God does all things for a good reason. Our suffering and pain is not, he insists, the direct result of divine punishment, nor divine manipulation in any other manner (evil, for example, as aspects of a divine tapestry, or a means for educational discipline, etc.). "Such answers are thought up by people," he insists, "who believe very strongly that God is a loving parent who controls what happens to us, and on the basis of that belief adjust and interpret the facts to fit their assumption."[18] "If God is testing us," he continues, then "He must know by now that many of us fail the test. If He is only giving burdens we {supposedly} can bear, I have seen Him miscalculate far too often."[19]

Kushner's non-traditional response is to argue that

God is limited in power, but not in goodness. God does not cause our suffering, despite the conventional teachings which (as we have seen) are sponsored still by evangelical theology and the Augustinian-Thomistic theodicy and which are endorsed by millions of Christians. Many people have found Kushner's answer less than reassuring, to be sure, but the fact that his book has sold hundreds of thousands of copies is testimony to the fact that, perhaps, the taking for granted of the traditional theodicy is no longer as simple for many people as it once was. It certainly has been questioned by professional theologians, and now by everyday Christians and Jews.

What is important to note here is that with the very real possibility of the collapse (if this is not too strong a word) of the traditional theodicy, the age-old solace and reassurance that everything happens for a divinely appointed reason also is at stake. This implies that a strange but genuine sense of comfort will be lost, despite the fact that the traditional understanding of God as fully in control of all events seemed to imply the disturbing conviction that God is less than loving in causing so much suffering, suffering which so often appears purely gratuitous, undeserved, and greatly out of proportion to the moral nature of the people who suffer. Without a God upon whom to attribute all evils, or at least who controls all events in order to ensure their meaningfulness in the ultimate scheme of things, people will have to take far more seriously personal responsibility for much of the world's evil, and may well be left wondering whether God can do much about it.

In focusing upon this question, the publication of Kushner's book has caused a theological furor, not so much among professional theologians (who have been familiar with the issue), but among media personnel and the masses of everyday Christians and Jews. As one recent commentator explains, Kushner's book "struck two deep but conflicting chords in our society. On the one hand . . . he has articulated a felt need in our time to dissociate God's hand not only from the massive forms of historical and social evil, but also from the personal tragedies that afflict individuals and families."[20] Kushner's central thesis, that (as he puts it) "I can worship a God who hates suffering but cannot eliminate it, more easily than I can worship a God who chooses to make children suffer and die,"[21] has exonerated God from being the cause of evil, and yet at the same time it has left an empty feeling in the hearts of a good many people who have been left wondering whether a God who is less than almighty is worthy of worship and whether the world is doomed to devour itself in evil.[22]

Kushner argues that evil "happens for no reason,"[23] that it is the result of randomness and bad luck, the callousness of other people, and the laws of nature which "treat everyone alike . . . {and which} do not make exceptions for good people or for useful people."[24] God has not created a perfect world, but a world wherein we are evolving slowly, with the pain and suffering we must endure as an inevitable consequence both of natural laws which we cannot control and also of human free will which itself causes much misery and anguish. God "will not intervene to take away our freedom, including our freedom to hurt ourselves and others around us."[25] Kushner's proposal is that the theodicy question is not, "why has God done this to me?" but, as Soelle and others have suggested, "how can I respond to this pain and tragedy?"[26]

The fact that Kushner's theodicy was written without the benefit of an informed academic exposure to other historical and contemporary theodicies mars his undeniably significant contribution. The book's main weakness clearly is a direct consequence of this unfamiliarity with professional scholarship. Kushner's insight that God is not all-powerful has been addressed in contemporary theological literature, and in comparison with these sophicated discussions, Kushner's seems very deficient. He does not tell us much about what God *does* do, i. e., *how* God acts in the world, except for a few brief comments about how God inspires us to act creatively and courageously.

(iii) Divine Power and a Suffering God

The writings on theodicy by many contemporary, professional theologians fill in this serious lacuna in Kushner's book.[27] Process theism, in particular, as we have seen (in *Chapter 6*), has argued for a drastic reinterpretation of divine omnipotence and has presented theological and metaphysical reasons for its necessity. Kushner's critics, who reject his God as too weak to be worthy of worship, seem unaware (or, in some cases, unconvinced) of the process theists' arguments that the conventional understanding of God as the sole, absolute power is problematic. The alternative concept of a "limited God" certainly seems offensive and psychologically threatening to traditional ears, yet process theists offer what many others consider to be substantial reasons against the viability of any other view.

Moltmann, moreover (see *Chapter 2*), and growing numbers of contemporary theologians of diverse backgrounds, have argued for a revised understanding of God which depicts the deity as far more compassionate than does the more traditional, conservative conception of an immutable and all-causative deity.

The biblical testimony, as we have seen (in *Chapter 3*), is ambivalent on this question, although early Christian theologians gradually came to agree that divine impassibility was to be the official and appropriate doctrine. This opinion was sanctioned by such historical giants as Augustine, Anselm and Aquinas, all of whom argued the point with great passion. The need among the common people, moreover, for such an impassive God seems undeniable, since it still seems unthinkable for most people to conceive of God in any other way.

The diverse and important arguments for and against the "suffering God" concept have been documented precisely in a recent book by Warren McWilliams, *The Passion of God's Divine Suffering in Contemporary Protestant Theology*.[28] He points out that there clearly is a strong and growing acknowledgment of the perception of God as a suffering companion, although many writers still resist the enticement to revise their conception of God from an all-powerful and immutable being to this suffering companion of the world's suffering creatures.

Richard Bauckham, among many others, also has pointed out this fact quite concisely in his useful analysis of the issue: "The idea that God cannot suffer, accepted virtually as axiomatic in Christian theology from the early Greek Fathers until the nineteenth century," he writes, has "in this century been progressively abandoned."[29] Ronald Goetz has affirmed much the same, although perhaps overstating the case: the "age-old dogma that God is impassible and immutable, incapable of suffering," he argues, "is for many no longer tenable. The ancient theopaschite heresy that God suffers has, in fact, become the new orthodoxy."[30]

H. M. Relton, moreover, fortuitously predicted as long ago as 1917 that there "are many indications that the doctrine of the suffering God is going to play a very prominent part in the theology of the age in which we live."[31] The historical background of this doctrine was surveyed in J. K. Mozley's 1926 work, *The Impassibility of God*,[32] and it is prominent in the writings of others like Nicholas Berdyaev, Kazoh Kitamori and Emil Brunner.[33]

There are a significant number of others (Schilling's research cites fifty theological exponents in addition to Mozley's twenty-two references),[34] including theologians of such diverse backgrounds and perspectives as Dietrich Bonhoeffer, James Cone (*and liberation theology in general*), Hans Küng, Rosemary Ruether (*and feminist theology in general*), William Temple, Daniel Day Williams, and Geddes MacGreggor.[35]

Terrence Fretheim, in his *The Suffering of God: An Old Testament Perspective*, has explored this significant issue from the perspective of biblical theology, making it clear that suffering irrefutably is part of the nature of purpose of God.[36] Claus Westermann[37] and Abraham Heschel, likewise, have made a similar point: "the most exalted idea applied to God" by the Hebrew prophets, Heschel argues, "is not infinite wisdom, infinite power, but infinite concern."[38] It is not "self-sufficiency," but rather "concern and involvement" which characterize God's relationship with the world.[39]

Process philosopher Lewis Ford has argued a similar point in his *The Lure of God: A Biblical Background for Process Theism*, contending that divine suffering and persuasive power are legitimate biblical themes, albeit themes which long have been overshadowed by the Hellenistic view of God as impassive and all-determining of earthly events.[40] It is process theology, more so than any other contemporary perspective, which has given weight to this new understanding of God. With it, we are witnessing an entirely new dimension of the theodicy issue, a dimension which has yet to be thoroughly exploited or fully appreciated.[41]

What concerns us here, most of all, of course, are the implications of this suffering God for the theodicy issue. It is no accident, as Richard Bauckham has pointed out, that the contemporary "concern with the question of divine suffering has frequently arisen out of situations in which suffering was acute":[42] English theologians responded to the devastation of the First World War, Japan's Kitamori responded to his experience of Hiroshima, Moltmann responded to Auschwitz, and the liberation movements (black liberation, feminism, etc.) are responding to the evil and suffering caused by social oppression and injustice.

It is incontrovertible that the denial of absolute, all-controlling power by God absolves the deity of responsibility for the evil and misery in the world. But the obvious question which arises is whether such a God can guarantee salvation and redemption. Goetz has addressed this question negatively: "{t}he doctrine that God is limited in power solves the problem {of evil} by sacrificing God's omnipotence," he contends, and the "concept of a limited deity finally entails a denial of the capacity of God to redeem the world, and thus, ironically, raises the question of whether God is in the last analysis even love."[43] Since God's ability to control the world is limited, Goetz insists, "then inescapably any other realm of being, any eschatological reality, would be similarly flawed."[44]

Moltmann's answer to this legitimate concern, however, has been to point out that while the suffering of God cannot prevent the world's misery and evil, it can and does help to transform the suffering: it heals the deepest aspect of human suffering: "godforsakenness."[45] Moltmann, moreover, has insisted that we cannot isolate the cross of Christ (the ultimate symbol of divine suffering) from the resurrection, for the resurrection is God's promise of liberation from suffering. A suffering God who is "vulnerable, takes suffering and death on himself in order to heal, to liberate and to confer new life," he insists. "The history of God's suffering in the passion of the Son and the sighings of the Spirit serves the history of God's joy in the Spirit and his completed felicity at the end. That is the ultimate goal of God's history of suffering in the world."[46]

Process theists, furthermore, argue that while God cannot coerce human events and hence cannot control in any absolute manner the goods and evils which befall us, the deity, nevertheless, is not to be perceived as helpless or any less worthy of worship. God's role, it is suggested, is to "lure" and persuade us all to seek value and meaning in every event, to actualize what is best for us at each impasse.

Schilling concurs: "God is constantly exploring and finding new ways of advance and creating new possibilities of value." God's power "reaches its apex in the compassionate love that takes to itself the agony and tragedy of the world and thereby heals and transforms it. It works primarily, not through fiat or the application of superior physical force, but through the anguished love that seeks the well-being even of those who oppose it."[47]

The suggestion put forth here is that we must learn to think of God's power as other than all-determining. The fact that we have been taught for centuries that God is all-powerful does not automatically and without debate render this understanding of God as the only valid interpretation of how God acts in the world. Indeed, the question of how God acts in the world is one of the most notoriously complex and enigmatic of theological problems. The newly proposed understanding of God as less than all-determining and indeed as a suffering companion, to be sure, is a radical shift in theological thinking, to say the least; it will not be accepted by the masses of Christian believers easily, accustomed as they are to a very different definition of God. Yet if the proponents of this newly proposed, revised theism are correct, a satisfactory solution to theodicy (or something like it) *may* be impossible without this alternative understanding of God.

9
Concluding Comments

The preponderance of evil and suffering has been the greatest threat to belief in the God defined by Christians as all-powerful and all-loving. Yet in our century, the incredible horror of the holocaust has given the theodicy issue a new and even more pressing urgency and significance. Among Jewish theologians in particular the trauma of the devastation has forced a serious reexamination of the relationship between God and evil.

In this final chapter, it seems appropriate and profitable to examine some of the leading Jewish theological responses to the holocaust, and then conclude this chapter and the book with a brief overview of the various theodicies (i. e., the scholars and themes) discussed in the preceding pages.

(i) Holocaust Theodicy

Moses Mendelssohn has stated that all history, including the holocaust, is God's doing: "All of this is *fact*—it must be part of the original design and must have been allowed for or at least included in wisdom's plan. Providence never fails to accomplish its goals."[1] There is, however, as we have seen, no consensus on this point. Richard

Rubenstein, to cite the most prominent Jewish example, has immense difficulty with the traditional interpretation, represented by Mendelssohn. In his oft-cited book, *After Auschwitz*,[2] Rubenstein has argued that the covenant God is obligated to punish evil, and that this punishment supposedly is just and deserved; yet, since this view implies that the Jews must bear responsibility for the holocaust, Rubenstein feels that he has no choice but to reject the God of the covenant: "To see any purpose in the death camps, the traditional believer is forced to regard the most demonic, antihuman explosion in all history as a meaningful expression of God's purposes."[3] Again, he writes: "The real objections against a personal or theistic God come from the irreconcilability of the claim of God's perfection with the hideous human evil tolerated by such a God. . . . A God who tolerates the suffering of even one innocent child is either infinitely cruel or hopelessly indifferent."[4] Rubenstein, like the philosopher-playwright, Camus, who influenced him, rejects the God of absolute power, since such an understanding of divine omnipotence is inconsistent with a world which has become so vicious and absurd.[5]

Other Jewish writers, nevertheless, have maintained their belief in the covenant relationship and have focused principally upon the following themes: disaster may be a test sent by God; suffering may be the result of a lack of group solidarity; and suffering may be a challenge of Jewish self-identification.[6]

Daniel Breslauer has suggested that these three elements usually have been examined in isolation and that each one has become a cornerstone for a different American Jewish theodicy. Eliezer Berkovits, for example, represents the first view:[7] after each catastrophe in Jewish history, God has done something new for the chosen ones: "through Israel God tested Western man and found him wanting."

Yet the holocaust, for Berkovits, is a testimony not only to the callousness of human beings but of the possibility of human self-transcendence.[8]

The second approach has major representatives in Emil Fackenheim[9] and Arthur Cohen,[10] among others: the holocaust creates the imperative for social conscience, for strengthening community. The third view, finally, represented by Maurice Friedman,[11] Irving Greenberg,[12] and others, interprets the holocaust as an opportunity whereby individuals can affirm and fulfil themselves.

There are other significant Jewish theodicies, explanations for the holocaust and other human miseries which range from conservative (traditional) perspectives to significantly novel proposals. Immanuel Hartom, for example, sees the holocaust as divine retribution for the sin of assimilation;[13] Joel Teitelbaum sees it as divine punishment for the sins of the Zionists;[14] Ignaz Maybaum claims that the Jews who died in the holocaust did so as vicarious suffering for the sins of others;[15] Martin Buber's well known view was that God is "eclipsed" or hidden, obscured by the intensity of suffering and evil;[16] and Maybaum appeals to the faith solution, conceding that God's ways simply are incomprehensible to us.[17]

Elie Wiesel speaks of a suffering God as an expression of divine goodness and love, despite the world's evil,[18] a view shared also by Abraham Heschel[19] and Hans Jonas. The latter insists, as do some of the writers discussed in the previous chapter, that we must seek to revise our understanding of God: "Auschwitz calls . . . the whole traditional concept of God into question."[20] In a manner consistent with process writers, Jonas contends that God is not omnipotent in the traditional sense, and indeed that the conventional concept of omnipotence is meaningless (logically, ontologically, and theologically).[21] Taken literally, "omnipotence" implies that God has all the power, and if this were the case, God's power would be power over nothing. Like process thinkers, Jonas insists that God *cannot* intervene to prevent evil and suffering. Unlike process thinkers, however, who offer metaphysical reasons for this conception of God, Jonas speaks only of "a God who for a time—the time of the ongoing world process—has divested himself of any power to interfere with the physical course of things."[22]

There certainly is no doubt that the holocaust has become our century's infamous symbol for evil. The diversity of viewpoints among the Jewish writers we have surveyed, moreover, attests to the fact that the problem of theodicy is as pressing and the answers as diverse as ever. The arguments of the Jewish theologians, furthermore, are not far removed from the Christian theodicies surveyed in this book, theodicies which range from the dominant, traditional (Augustinian-Thomistic) stance to the innovative proposals found, for example, in Hick's Irenaean theodicy and in the revised understanding of divine power and in the innovative emphasis upon divine suffering.

There clearly is no unanimity on this issue, and yet it does appear that the traditional Augustinian-Thomistic theodicy, the mainstay of Catholic theology and conservative Protestantism as well, is being challenged in significant and provocative ways by the creative proposals of many contemporary theists, Jewish and Christian alike. The challenge is to rethink the entire theodicy issue and certainly the key issue concerning our understanding of God and how God acts in the world.

(ii) Moral and Physical Evil: An Overview

As we have seen, the two fundamental theodicy questions, that of reconciling moral evil and physical evil with belief in God, have been examined by various theologians and philosophers in a number of ways.

Moral evil, to be sure, is explained as the consequence of the misuse and abuse of human freedom: there seems to be no other likely explanation. The issue, of course, is whether any of the diverse formulations of the free will solution are viable. The biblical record, as we have seen, clearly emphasized divine controlling power, even though there are many biblical passages which assume the authenticity of human freedom vis-à-vis this divine power. Augustine's uniquely influential theodicy, moreover, based the free will solution on the certainty of human free will; and yet, at the same time, he proposed a conception of God (and an understanding of Adam and Eve and their "original sin," passed on to their progeny) which seems to many contemporary theists to negate, rather than be congruous with, human freedom. Augustine's doctrine of divine predestination, supported quite vehemently by the Protestant reformers, likewise appears to many contemporary theologians to be problematic since, again, it seems to deny the validity of human free will.

Aquinas, nonetheless, offered sophisticated arguments for the authenticity of our freedom vis-à-vis divine causal agency in the world, arguments which have been elaborated and defended by contemporary Thomists. Plantinga's free will defense, moreover, was formulated to demonstrate that evil is *not* incoherent with the existence of God, and Hick's theodicy argues for the necessity of an imperfect world as the means to a sound free will defense (for creatures otherwise could not genuinely be free). Process thinkers go even further by insisting upon the necessity of freedom (in distinction to the traditional view, shared by Hick and most other Christian theologians, that freedom is a gift, a self-limiting by God of some of the deity's power) and by rejecting other versions of the free will defense as being undermined by the traditional understanding of divine power.

The revised theism which conceives of the deity as less than all-controlling in power and as a suffering companion is becoming more widespread, popularized by Kushner and utilized by many Jewish theologians and especially by process thinkers, among growing numbers of other Christian writers who are responding to the horrors of the holocaust and the awesome devastation and injustices perpetrated in this century.

The question of *natural evil* and its relationship to a good and powerful God, as we have noted, always has been an equally difficult, if indeed not a more difficult, problem to answer. Traditional theodicy often accounted for such evil as the result of divine punishment, or as tests of faith— "acts of God," given to us by God for a justifiable, yet ultimately unknowable, reason. Aquinas and others, furthermore, have advanced the view that the necessity of natural laws to support human life accounts for natural evils as unfortunate, yet necessary, side-effects.

The aesthetic theory, moreover, argues that what may appear to us to be evil in the parts of creation may in fact be necessary parts of a good whole. Process theists use the aesthetic theory in a very different manner, arguing that every creaturely experience has some aesthetic value. This explanation of natural evil challenges the view of many contemporary writers that some evil is purely gratuitous.[23] Riechenbach argues, furthermore, that natural evils are inherent, and necessarily so, in the system of natural laws which supports human life, and Swinburne contends that natural evils are, in fact, a necessary condition for human free will.

There are other significant perspectives on this question of natural evil which have not been addressed in this short book. One of these must be mentioned here, if only in passing. There are many contemporary theologians who find the question of *animal suffering* to be at the center of any inquiry about natural evil, and who find this to be an issue which has not been confronted adequately in the historical theodicies nor, indeed, in the overwhelming majority of the contemporary theodicies, traditional or innovative.

Conventional theodicy seems to suggest little more than that animal suffering (and natural evil in general) is the result of human sin, although the age-old "principle of plenitude" suggests that God created all possible levels of existence and that each particular species makes a valuable contribution to the perfection of the whole. But these traditional positions are being challenged more and more as unjustifiable, anthropocentric speculations. John Stuart Mill long ago argued that animal suffering is a significant argument against belief in a loving deity: "If there are any marks at all of special design in creation," he wrote sarcastically, "one of the things most evidently designed is that a large proportion of animals should pass their existence in tormenting and devouring other animals."[24]

Among the contemporary writers who are addressing the issue of animal suffering, the most prominent may be Peter Singer and Tom Regan.[25] Singer argues strongly against what he calls "speciesism," the view that people treat the interests of human beings as more important than those of non-human life, "non-human animals" in particular. This conviction, he insists, has led to the morally indefensible practice of rearing and killing animals (cruelly indeed, yet also if it is done painlessly) for food and for laboratory experiments.

A number of other philosophers also have been arguing that animals (or at least some of them) have moral rights.[26] The arguments and counter-arguments are complex, but essentially the reasoning of animal-rights advocates is that since animals, like human beings, have interests and can suffer pain, they have the same moral right as humans have to protection from pain and the right from harmful interference by human beings. The fact that animals do not possess rationality, an autonomous will or a concept of the self (and hence, as the opponents say, are not moral agents with legitimate claims to moral rights), supposedly is irrelevant: certain human beings lack these same capacities—infants, for example, and the severely retarded—and yet they are granted the moral rights in question.

What concerns us here are the implications of animal suffering for the theodicy issue: the question as to whether or not animals have rights is intriguing and relevant, yet not one we can hope to settle. Our interest is with theologians like Hick (to cite one prominent example) who have been criticized for explaining animal pain as part of the environment which is necessary for there to be human "soul-making," and who then regard animals suffering as "subordinate to that of {the question} of human sin and suffering."[27]

Hick defends his view, however, by insisting that pain serves animals, as it does humans, as a biological warning device of external danger: pain is a necessary part of our "equipment for survival."[28] He suggests, moreover, that while it appears certain that higher animals do feel pain, lower invertebrates "which have no central nervous system at all" probably have no conscious experiences of pain. Pain and death, furthermore, may not be a profound problem even for the higher animals since animals do not experience the anticipation of death and mental torments in the way human beings most assuredly do.[29] Hick probably would argue (as C. S. Lewis and others have) that it is a clear instance of the "pathetic fallacy" to believe that animals feel as human beings do.[30] Hick has proposed also (with reservations and qualifications) that animal suffering might be understood somewhat in the light of the Hindu-Buddhist understanding of reincarnation: all life forms an organic whole, with higher beings continually evolving from lower life forms.[31] Hindu and Buddhist stories contain many references to past lives of human beings wherein people were incarnated as animals and birds and even as inanimate objects; there are also Indian scriptural passages which speak of reincarnations as animals and other non-human life forms as just punishment for human sins.

(iii) Evil and the Experience of Life's Goodness

What, then, are we to make of the problem of evil? That the world contains immense suffering and misery is undeniable, and yet it seems highly doubtful whether our best theological minds, despite the continuing discussions, will ever solve the riddle as to *why* God allows such evil or, in different words, *how* evil (human and non-human) is reconcilable with belief in God. We must remember, nevertheless, that while the world's creatures suffer from terrible anguish, there is (for human beings at least) another aspect of reality which can and does sustain us, *despite* the evil. There is much in life to celebrate, much which can instill in us an optimistic sense of well-being and confidence. We are fortunate indeed, for example, if we have experienced those graced moments of serene beauty while walking in a dampened forest or by feeling the peace and majesty of the open sea; or, again, if we have been deeply moved and comforted somehow by the awesome and mysterious vault of the star-filled heavens on a quiet evening, or shared the joys of intimate friendship and the indescribable love of a parent for our children. Such moments are to be cherished, for they somehow sustain us and assure us that we are in communion with a Presence which animates all life by its care and concern. They bear testimony to a "peace which passes all understanding."

The teachings of the great prophets and the testimony of mystics (like St. John of the Cross, for instance, and others like Thomas Merton, Simone Weil and St. Teresa) burst with references to these experiences. Those of us who are not mystics can, at the very least, make use of their witness and appropriate some of their insights into the spiritual dimension of reality in order to help us find much needed encouragement and comfort in our darker moments. Mystical confirmations of a loving Presence, a Presence which pervades the universe and which resides within our very souls, reassure and console us that life indeed is good, despite the evil and suffering we must endure.[32] The evil is not rendered any less real or any less evil, but it is seen from a much broader and more adequate perspective whenever we are cognizant of life's goodness.

(iv) Evil, Miracles and Faith

Relevant to the theodicy issue is the following highly contentious point which we have addressed in various contexts in the preceding chapters. Many contemporary theologians are suggesting that we cannot expect the world to be manipulated by God though intermittent and sporadic acts of divine intervention in order to cure this particular case of cancer or that particular natural disaster. Traditional theology, of course, maintains the belief that since God is the primary actor in this world drama, God most certainly *can* perform miracles (and so-called faith healings[33]). Yet, many contemporary theologians are advising that while

God *can* perform miracles, God does *not* do so for some very good reasons.[34] Others, like the process theologians, go even further in contending that God *cannot* perform miracles to prevent suffering, but must endure evil and misery along with us as a fellow-sufferer; God, nonetheless, as process theists insist, continuously persuades us and grants us the strength and grace to experience the most aesthetic value and meaning which is possible within every experience, no matter how bleak some experiences may be.

The question of miracles, of course, is tied up intricately with our understanding of *God's power*, and there are various opinions and perspectives regarding what miracles are: can God violate natural laws by performing miracles from time to time, or are miracles not better understood as the "religious experience" of God working within natural laws, laws which may or may not be understood fully by us?[35]

Perhaps faith in God is all we have, despite the evil and misery in the world. Yet our faith is far more likely to survive and grow if we make a decisive effort to cultivate a critical and informed faith. The problem of evil, of course, challenges our faith and well-being more so than any other concern; yet, as we have seen, the writings of some of the greatest theological and philosophical minds have sought (and will continue to seek) to formulate some answers to this most terrible of mysteries. Theological writings aspire to clarify which solutions to the theodicy puzzle are inadequate and which are the most beneficial and promising, in order that we may better cope with life's unfairness and the tragedies which strike us all with such devastating and bewildering force.

There will be no final solution to this problem, but there certainly has been a furor of theological deliberation and renewed interest in this issue during the past few decades. New understandings of God and God's causal activity in the world, and new understandings of God's relationship to evil, as we have seen, are being proposed and hotly debated. Hopefully, the quality of our lives will be altered by these important discussions, for the questions they address are the very questions which most adversely affect the very meaningfulness and the significance of our lives.

Notes

Chapter 1

1. The term "theodicy" was coined by the eighteenth century German philosopher, Gottfried Wilhelm Leibniz. The word is based on the conflation of the Greek words "theos" (God) and "diké" (justice). Theodicy, then, is the attempt to affirm divine justice despite the suffering in the world, suffering which so often seems arbitrary and gratuitous. Leibniz wrote his famous book, *Theodicy: Essays on the Goodness of God, the Freedom of Man, and the Origin of Evil*, in 1710.

2. Shalom J. Kahn has argued that all great literature is profoundly moral in its implications and that the central problem in literature of all kinds always has been the theme of good and evil: see his insightful article, "The Problem of Evil in Literature," *Journal of Aesthetics and Art Criticism* (1953), 98–110.

3. Karl Rahner, "Why Does God Allow Us to Suffer?" in his *Theological Investigations, XIX* (New York: Crossroad, 1983), 194.

4. See, for example, John Bowker's *Problems of Suffering in Religions of the World* (Cambridge: Cambridge University Press, 1970). See also Arthur Herman's *The Problem of Evil and Indian Thought* (Delhi: Motilal Bararsidass, 1976).

5. David Hume, *Dialogues Concerning Natural Religion* (originally published in 1779), Norman Kemp Smith, ed. (New York: Bobbs-Merrill Co., Inc., 1947), 198.

6. For this, among other things, Hume is often referred to

as the "patron saint of skeptics," yet the theodicy issue has been a perceived threat to belief in God since at least the time of Epicurus (341–270 B.C.). See Paul Schilling's discussion of this point in his exceptionally useful book, *God and Human Anguish* (Nashville: Abingdon Press, 1977), 38. See also John Hick's discussion in his classic book, *Evil and the God of Love*, second edition (New York: Harper and Row, 1978), 5. Epicurus formulated the theodicy issue as follows:

> God either wishes to take away evils, and is unable; or He is able, and is unwilling; or He is neither willing nor able, or He is both willing and able. If He is willing and is unable, He is feeble, which is not in accordance with the character of God; if He is able and unwilling, He is envious, which is equally at variance with God; if He is neither willing nor able, He is both envious and feeble, and therefore not God; if He is both willing and able, which alone is suitable to God, from what source then are evils? or why does He not remove them? (*On the Anger of God*, in *The Writings of the Ante-Nicene Fathers* {Grand Rapids: Eerdmans, 1951}, Chapter 13, Volume 7).

7. Among them are philosophers like Antony Flew, H. D. Aiken, John Mackie, J. Ducasse, W. T. Stace, J. E. McTaggart, and H. J. McCloskey. Nelson Pike has documented this discussion in his essay, "Hume on Evil," in Nelson Pike, ed., *God and Evil* (Englewood Cliffs, N. J. : Prentice-Hall, 1964), 86–87.

8. C. S. Lewis, *The Problem of Pain* (London: Collins, 1940), 14.

9. Nelson Pike, "Hume on Evil," 86–87.

10. Augustine formulated the theodicy issue as follows:

> Behold God, and behold what God hath created; and God is good, most mightily and incomparably better than all these; but yet He, who is good, hath created

them good. . . . Where, then, is evil, and whence, and
how crept it in hither? What is its root, and what its
seed? Or has it no being at all? Why, then, do we face
and shun that which has no being? . . . He, indeed, the
greatest and chiefest Good, has created these lesser
goods, but both Creator and created are all good.
Whence is evil? (from Augustine's *Confessions, VII,* 5
{New York: The Modern Library, 1949}).

See Schilling's discussion of this point in his *God and Human
Anguish,* 38–39.

11. See C. S. Lewis, *The Problem of Pain,* 77; Hick, *Evil and
the God of Love,* 263; and Aquinas, who wrote: "Things which
are generated and corrupted, in which alone there can be natural
evil, are a very small part of the whole universe" (*Summa Theologica, I,* Question 49, Art. 3, Reply Obj. 5). See Schilling, *God
and Human Anguish,* 27–28.

12. Hume, *Dialogues Concerning Natural Religion,* 195–
196.

13. See Dostoevski, "Rebellion," in Pike, ed., *God and Evil,*
6–16.

14. G. H. Joyce, *Principles of Natural Theology* (New York:
Longmans, 1972), 584.

15. Hume, *Dialogues Concerning Natural Religion,* 194.

Chapter 2

1. John Hick, *Evil and the God of Love,* second edition
(New York: Harper and Row, 1978), 11.

2. Nelson Pike, "Hume on Evil," in Nelson Pike, ed., *God
and Evil* (Englewood Cliffs, N. J. : Prentice-Hall, 1964), 88.

3. Karl Rahner, "Why Does God Allow Us to Suffer?" in
his *Theological Investigations, XIX* (New York: Crossroad,
1983), 206.

4. Rahner, "Why Does God Allow Us to Suffer?" 208.

5. John Cobb, "The Problem of Evil and the Task of Min-

istry," in Stephen Davis, ed., *Encountering Evil* (Atlanta: John Knox, 1981), 176.

6. Simone Weil, *Waiting on God* (London: Collins, 1950), 80.

7. Cited in Paul Schilling, *God and Human Anguish* (Nashville: Abingdon, 1977), 66–67.

8. Paul Schilling, *God and Human Anguish*, 70–73.

9. Ian Barbour, *Myths, Models, and Paradigms* (New York: Harper and Row, 1974), 137.

10. C. S. Lewis, *A Grief Observed* (New York: Bantam, 1976), 25.

11. Lewis, *A Grief Observed*, 29.

12. Lewis, *A Grief Observed*, 29.

13. There are many excellent discussions of the problem of evil from this existential perspective. See, for example, Wayne and Charles Oates, *People in Pain: Guidelines for Pastoral Care* (Philadelphia: Westminster Press, 1985); Philip Yancey, *Where Is God When It Hurts?* (Grand Rapids: Zondervan, 1977); Sara Kay Cohen, *Whoever Said Life Is Fair?* (New York: Berkeley Books, 1977); Michael Peterson, *Evil and the Christian God* (Grand Rapids: Baker Book House, 1982), 135–154; Schilling's *God and Human Anguish*, 29–54; and Kenneth Surin, *Theology and the Problem of Evil* (Oxford: Blackwell, 1986), 112–141.

14. John Bowker, *Problems of Suffering in Religions of the World* (New York: Cambridge University Press, 1970), 2.

15. Brian Hebblethwaite, *Evil, Suffering, and Religion* (London: Sheldon Press, 1976), 14–39.

16. Dorothee Soelle, *Suffering* (Philadelphia: Fortress Press, 1975).

17. Jürgen Moltmann, *The Crucified God*, translated by R. A. Wilson and John Bowden (London: SCM Press, 1974).

18. Jürgen Moltmann, *The Experiment Hope*, translated by M. Douglas Meeks (London: SCM, 1975), 83.

19. Jürgen Moltmann, *Theology of Hope* (New York: Harper and Row, 1967).

20. Moltmann, *The Crucified God*, 277.

21. Kenneth Surin, *Theology and the Problem of Evil*, 131.

22. Hick, *Evil and the God of Love*, 7–9.

23. Hick, *Evil and the God of Love*, 244, 8.

24. Peterson, *Evil and the Christian God*, 40.

25. Peterson, *Evil and the Christian God*, 42. Peterson documents the testimonies of John Bowker, Max Weber, William James, Talcot Parsons and A. R. King, all of whom have defined the theodicy question as an existential one.

26. Peterson, *Evil and the Christian God,* 42.

Chapter 3

1. Daniel Simundson, *Faith Under Fire* (Minneapolis: Augsburg, 1980), 15.

2. E. S. Gerstenberger and W. Schrage, *Suffering* (Nashville: Abingdon, 1977), 132.

3. Gerstenberger and Schrage, *Suffering*, 206.

4. See Gerstenberger and Schrage, *Suffering*: "The New Testament . . . in spite of the fact that it . . . is acquainted with human action as causing suffering, can just as definitely identify God himself or his will as the cause of suffering" (236). Schrage points out, however, that this view is softened and qualified somewhat in the New Testament.

5. D. A. Carson, *Divine Sovereignty and Human Responsibility* (Atlanta: John Knox Press, 1981). See also the universally acclaimed work of one of my former teachers, E. P. Sanders: *Paul and Palestinian Judaism* (Philadelphia: Fortress, 1977). Carson's critical exposition of Sanders' work largely is sympathetic and helpful for the non-specialist. He criticizes Sanders for not being sufficiently aware of the changing historical face of the sovereignty-responsibility tension. A detailed account of this developmental aspect is the strength of Carson's work.

6. Carson, *Divine Sovereignty and Human Responsibility*, 38.

7. Carson, *Divine Sovereignty and Human Responsibility*, 24.

8. See, for example, David Griffin's important discussion in his *God, Power and Evil* (Philadelphia: Westminster Press, 1976).

9. James Barr has written a number of books on this point. See, for example, his *Fundamentalism* (Philadelphia: Westminster Press, 1977), *Escaping From Fundamentalism* (London: SCM, 1984), and *The Bible in the Modern World* (New York: Harper and Row, 1973). See also Rudolph Bultmann's *Jesus Christ and Mythology* (New York: Charles Scribner's Sons, 1958), *Theology of the New Testament* (New York: Charles Scribner's Sons, 1951 and 1955), etc. See also John Sanford's *Evil, The Shadow Side of Reality* (New York: Crossroad, 1981), and William Duggan's *Myth and Christian Belief* (Notre Dame: Fides, 1971).

10. John Hick, *Evil and the God of Love*, second edition (New York: Harper and Row, 1978), 210.

11. F. D. Fohr, *Adam and Eve: The Spiritual Symbolism of Genesis and Exodus* (Landam, MD: University Press of America, 1986).

12. See the study of Charles Hummel, *The Galileo Connection* (Downers Grove, IL: Intervarsity Press, 1986). Hummel points out that about sixty percent of the Old Testament is historical narrative, but that the remaining forty percent is religious interpretation. The same proportion applies to the New Testament.

13. See, for example, Alvin Plantinga's writings: *The Nature of Necessity* (Oxford: Clarendon Press, 1974), *God, Freedom, and Evil* (New York: Harper and Row, 1974), *God and Other Minds* (Ithaca, New York: Cornell University Press, 1967). Plantinga exploits Augustine's argument which attributes much of the evil in the world to Satan, or to Satan and his cohorts. Plantinga argues that this need not be true in a literal sense; it is required only that the postulation of Satan as responsible for much of the world's natural evil is a possibility. See also Stephen Davis, *Logic and the Nature of God* (Grand Rapids, MI: Eerdmans, 1983), 112–114.

Other writers, rather than locating the evil power in a being (Satan) which exists outside of God, locate evil within God. Frederick Sontag, for example, teaches that within the divine being, God "combines and balances a number of forces, both good and malignant" (*The God of Evil: An Argument for the Existence of the Devil* {New York: Harper and Row, 1970}, 129, etc.). See also his *God, Why Did You Do That?* (Philadelphia: Westminster Press, 1970). Schilling's critique of this type of "dualism" is instructive: see his *God and Human Anguish* (Nashville: Abingdon, 1977), 115–118.

14. Paul Schilling, *God and Human Anguish*, 110.

15. See Schilling, *God and Human Anguish*, 108–113; Gerstenberger and Schrage, *Suffering*, 113–115 and 239–242; and the *Encyclopedic Dictionary of the Bible* (New York: McGraw-Hill, 1963), 2134–2137.

16. Schilling, *God and Human Anguish*, 111–114.

17. There are numerous biblical references to this theme. God punished Adam and Eve for their sin (Gen 3:16–19) and later destroyed much of the world with the great flood as punishment for human sinfulness (Gen 6–9). The success or failure of Israel's crops and her battles, moreover, was interpreted as either divine punishment or blessings. Jeremiah, for example, attributed the fall of Jerusalem to the sin of God's chosen people (Jer 44:22–23), and Job's "comforters" assured him that his suffering was due to divine punishment (Job 4:7–8). Paul taught us that "a man reaps what he sows" (Gal 6:7–8) and Matthew's Christ advises us that the poor tree which yields bad fruit "is cut down and burnt" (Mt 7:18–19). For other references, see Barry Whitney, *Evil and the Process God* (New York: Edwin Mellen Press, 1985), 25–28; Gerstenberger and Schrage, *Suffering*, 227–231; and Schilling, *God and Human Anguish*, 119–145.

18. There are many biblical references to this theme. See Whitney, *Evil and the Process God*, 182; Gerstenberger and Schrage, *Suffering*, 107; Daniel Simundson, *Faith Under Fire*, 55–61, etc.

19. Klaus Koch, "Is There a Doctrine of Retribution in the Old Testament?" in James Crenshaw, ed., *Theodicy in the Old Testament* (Philadelphia: Fortress Press, 1983), 57–87.

20. W. Brueggemann, "Theodicy in a Social Dimension," *Journal for the Study of the Old Testament* (1985), 3–25.

21. Crenshaw, "The Shift from Theodicy to Anthropodicy," in Crenshaw, ed., *Theodicy in the Old Testament*, 1–16.

22. See, for example, Griffin, *God, Power, and Evil,* and Whitney, *Evil and the Process God.*

23. There are many biblical references to this theme. The author of the First Letter of Peter, for example, sees suffering as a test of faith, much as gold is tested as it "passes through the assayer's fire" (1 Pet 1:6–7). For a discussion of this theme, see Whitney, *Evil and the Process God,* 28–30; Gerstenberger and Schrage, *Suffering,* 215–218.

A closely related theme explains evil as divine educational discipline: "it is only through his own pain that man learns to stay within his limits and thereby to provide a basis for his happiness" (Gerstenberger and Schrage, *Suffering,* 110). See also Simundson, *Faith Under Fire,* 130–132 and Whitney, *Evil and the Process God,* 182–183.

24. James Crenshaw, *A Whirlpool of Torment* (Philadelphia: Fortress Press, 1984).

25. See, for example, Crenshaw, "The Shift from Theodicy to Anthropodicy," 8.

26. Simundson, *Faith Under Fire,* 68.

27. Gerstenberger and Schrage, *Suffering,* 181–182.

28. Simundson, *Faith Under Fire,* 131–132.

29. See Simundson, *Faith Under Fire,* 133.

30. See Ronald Williams, "Current Trends in the Study of the Book of Job," in Walter Aufrecht, ed., *Studies in the Book of Job* (Waterloo, Ontario: Canadian Corporation for Studies in Religion, 1985), 2.

31. Crenshaw, "The Shift from Theodicy to Anthropodicy," 7.

Chapter 4

1. See John Hick, *Evil and the God of Love,* second edition (New York: Harper and Row, 1978), 246.

2. Charles Journet, *The Meaning of Evil* (P. J. Kenedy and Sons, 1963), 33. The reference is to Augustine's *Confessions,* Book III, Chapter 7, No. 12.

3. See Hick, *Evil and the God of Love,* 182ff.

4. See Hick, *Evil and the God of Love*, 181.

5. See Hick, *Evil and the God of Love*, 187.

6. Hick, *Evil and the God of Love*, 94–95. The reference is to Aquinas, *Summa Theologica*, translated by the Fathers of the English Dominican Province (London: R. and T. Washbourne Ltd., 1912) Part I, Question xlvii, Article 1.

7. Hick, *Evil and the God of Love*, 95. The reference is to Aquinas, *Summa Theologica*, Part 1, Question xxv, Article 6.

8. See Griffin's discussion in his *God, Power, and Evil* (Philadelphia: Westminster, 1976), 85. The text cited is from Aquinas, *Summa Contra Gentiles* (sometimes called *On the Truth of the Catholic Faith*).

9. Austin Farrer, *Love Almighty and Ills Unlimited* (London: Collins, 1966), 50. See Peter Hare and Edward Madden, *Evil and the Concept of God* (Springfield, IL: Charles C. Thomas, 1968), 66–69, for a critical discussion of this theme.

10. There are many writings on this theme. See, for example, Robert Burch, "The Defence from Plenitude Against the Problem of Evil," *International Journal for Philosophy of Religion* (1981), 29–37; G. Stanley Kane, "Evil and Privation," *International Journal for Philosophy of Religion* (1980), 43–58; Paul Thelakat, "Process and Privation: Aquinas and Whitehead on Evil," *International Philosophical Quarterly* (1986), 289–296; Bill Anglin and Stewart Goetz, "Evil as Privation," *International Journal for Philosophy of Religion* (1982), 3–12; etc.

11. Edward Madden and Peter Hare, *Evil and the Concept of God* (Springfield, IL: C. C. Thomas, 1968), 68–69.

12. See Hick, *Evil and the God of Love*, 70–82.

13. The text cited is from Aquinas' *Treatise on the Incarnation*. See Jacques Maritain's discussion in his *Saint Thomas and the Problem of Evil* (Milwaukee: Marquette University Press, 1942) and his *God and the Permission of Evil* (Milwaukee: Bruce Publishing Company, 1966).

14. Journet, *The Meaning of Evil*, 91, 114–118.

15. Karl Rahner, "Why Does God Allow Us to Suffer?" in his *Theological Investigations, XIX* (New York: Crossroad, 1983), 198.

16. See the discussion in *Chapter 7.*

17. Journet, *The Meaning of Evil,* 77–86.

18. Maritain, *God and the Permission of Evil,* 1 (note 2), etc.

19. Griffin, *God, Power and Evil,* 87–88.

20. Maritain, *God and the Permission of Evil,* 37.

21. Maritain, *God and the Permission of Evil,* 63.

22. See, for example, Maurice Wiles, "Farrer's Concept of Double Agency," *Theology* (1981), 243–249.

23. Austin Farrer, *Faith and Speculation* (London: Adam and Charles Black, 1967), 104.

24. For a useful critique of Farrer's use of this theme see Wiles, "Farrer's Concept of Double Agency."

25. Rahner, "Why Does God Allow Us to Suffer?" 196.

26. An effective critique of this theme is found in an article by Fred Berthold: "Free Will and Theodicy in Augustine: An Exposition and Critique," *Religious Studies* (1981), 525–535. There are numerous writings on the free will defense, be it Augustine's version or other versions: see note 30.

27. Augustine, *On Free Will,* III, 48 in John H. S. Burleigh, translator, *Augustine's Earlier Writings* (London: SCM Press, 1953), 200. See also Augustine, *Confessions, VII* (New York: The Modern Library, 1949), 122.

28. Journet, *The Meaning of Evil,* 184.

29. Journet, *The Meaning of Evil,* 184.

30. There are a great many writings on the free will defense. Among them are the important writings of Alvin Plantinga: *God and Other Minds* (Ithaca: Cornell University Press, 1967), *God, Freedom and Evil* (New York: Harper and Row, 1974), and *The Nature of Necessity* (Oxford: Clarendon Press, 1974). Austin Farrer's *The Freedom of the Will* (New York: Harper and Row, 1974) is a classic presentation. Other especially relevant writings include the following: Theodore Konoleon, "The Free Will Defense: New and Old," *Thomist* (1983), 1–42; James Tomberlin and Frank McGuinness, "God, Evil, and the Free Will Defence," *Religious Studies* (1977), 455–475; Robert Ackerman, "An Alternative Free Will Defence," *Religious Studies* (1982), 365–372; G. Stanley Kane, "The Free-Will Defence Defended," *New Scholas-*

ticism (1976), 435–446; William Wainwright, *International Journal for Philosophy of Religion* (1975), 243–250; David Basinger, "Human Freedom and Divine Providence: Some New Thoughts on an Old Problem," *Religious Studies* (1979), 491–510; Nelson Pike, "Plantinga on Free Will and Evil," *Religious Studies* (1979), 449–473; John Mackie, "Evil and Omnipotence," in Nelson Pike, ed., *God and Evil* (Englewood Cliffs, New Jersey: Prentice-Hall, 1964), 355–344; Antony Flew, "Divine Omnipotence and Human Freedom," in Antony Flew and A. MacIntyre, eds., *New Essays in Philosophical Theology* (London: SCM Press, 1955), 144–169; Stephen Davis, "A Defence of the Free Will Defence," *Religious Studies* (1972), 335–343; Frank Dilley, "Is the Free Will Defence Irrelevant?" *Religious Studies* (1982), 355–364; etc.

31. See the critical discussions on this theme by Griffin in *God, Power, and Evil*, 101–130.

32. See Hick, *Evil and the God of Love*, 64–69.

33. Augustine, *On the Predestination of the Saints, XXII*, in *Basic Writings of St. Augustine*, 797.

34. See Griffin, *God, Power, and Evil*, 81–82.

35. Journet, *The Meaning of Evil*, 176–177.

36. Journet, *The Meaning of Evil*, 178.

37. Jacques Maritain, *Freedom in the Modern World* (London: Sheed and Ward, 1935), 81–82. Journet cites this text with approval in his *The Meaning of Evil*, 179.

38. See Austin Farrer, *The Freedom of the Will*. For valuable discussions of Farrer's views, see Hebblethwaite's "Providence and Divine Action," *Religious Studies* (1979), 223–236; and *For God and Clarity: New Essays in Honor of Austin Farrer*, Jeffrey Eaton and Ann Loades, eds. (Allison Park, PA: Pickwick Publications, 1983).

39. Farrer, "Grace and Freewill," in his *Faith and Speculation* (London: Adam and Charles Black, 1967), 52–67.

40. Farrer, "Grace and Freewill," 66. For a critical discussion of this point, see Wiles, "Farrer's Concept of Double Agency."

41. This is Hebblethwaite's comment: see his article "Free-

dom, Evil and Farrer," 182. Farrer's theodicy book, *Love Almighty and Ills Unlimited* (London: Collins, 1962) is concerned almost solely with natural evil.

42. Rahner, "Why Does God Allow Us to Suffer?" 201.

43. Rahner, "Why Does God Allow Us to Suffer?" 202.

44. Rahner, interestingly enough, has defended the free will of human beings within the corpus of his voluminous writings. The question, of course, is whether or not he has been able to do so in a manner consistent with his understanding of divine causal action in the world.

45. Rahner, "Why Does God Allow Us to Suffer?" 206. See also Rahner's "The Human Question of Meaning in the Face of the Absolute Mystery of God," *Theological Investigations, XVIII* (New York: Crossroad, 1983), 89–104.

Chapter 5

1. Hick, *Evil and the God of Love*, second edition (New York: Harper and Row, 1978), 202.

2. The origin of this term is the poet, John Keats. See Schilling's explanation in his *God and Human Anguish* (Nashville: Abingdon Press, 1977), 146–147.

3. Berdyaev's theodicy contains many complex components, yet we may note (in particular) his understanding of the struggle for good as presupposing the existence of, and encounter with, evil. For a full account, see his *Spirit and Reality* (London: Geoffrey Bles, 1939) and *Freedom and the Spirit* (New York: Charles Scribner's Sons, 1939). Schilling offers a useful exposition of Berdyaev's main points in *God and Human Anguish*, 151–154.

4. See Radoslav Tsanoff, *The Nature of Evil* (New York: The Macmillan Company, 1931). Schilling provides a good summary of Tsanoff's position in *God and Human Anguish*, 155–157.

5. See F. R. Tennant, *Philosophical Theology*, 2 volumes (Cambridge: The University Press, 1930). The world is a place for moral growth, he confirms, growth which is attained by the overcoming of evil. Again, see Schilling's summary exposition of

the main points of Tennant's theodicy in *God and Human Anguish*, 157–160.

6. Farrer's theodicy contains elements of the "character-building" solution. See his *Love Almighty and Ills Unlimited* (London: Collins, 1966).

7. See, for example, Teilhard's *On Suffering* (New York: Harper and Row, 1974) and *The Phenomenon of Man* (New York: Harper, 1959). Teilhard espouses the view that God created an imperfect universe, one which is evolving toward God (the Omega point) via the overcoming of evil and the making of our spiritual natures. Teilhard's theodicy also shares themes both with the traditional Augustinian-Thomistic theodicy and with the process theodicy of Whitehead, Hartshorne and Griffin. With the traditional theodicy, he identified evil with non-being; yet he believed that evil theoretically ceases to be a scandal when it is considered in a world of becoming (see Michael H. Murray, *The Thought of Teilhard de Chardin* {New York: Seabury Press, 1966}, 95). With Whiteheadian process theodicy, Teilhard shares the view that all life is "becoming" or evolving; yet while Whiteheadian thought sees the world as *processing* continually without ever reaching an end, Teilhard espouses the view that all life *progresses* toward God and finally will be spiritually perfected (as Hick holds), if humans beings are able to respond to divine grace and thereby overcome evil.

8. See Hick, *Evil and the God of Love*, 65, 203–204.

9. See Hick, *Evil and the God of Love*, 220. Hick refers here to Schleiermacher, the eighteenth century German theologian who was among the first to outline an Irenaean-type theodicy.

10. See Hick, "An Irenaean Theodicy," in Stephen Davis, ed., *Encountering Evil* (Atlanta: John Knox Press, 1981), 42. Hick acknowledges that this Irenaean distinction is a misinterpretation of Genesis, but its implications for a two-stage creation are, he insists, quite valid.

11. Hick, "An Irenaean Theodicy," 42.

12. Hick, "An Irenaean Theodicy," 43.

13. See *Chapter 7* and also Hick, *Evil and the God of Love*, 267–271.

14. Hick, "An Irenaean Theodicy," 44.

15. See Hick, *Evil and the God of Love*, 270–271. Smart's essay, "Omnipotence, Evil and Supermen," *Philosophy* (1961), has been the source of much discussion. It is reprinted in Nelson Pike, ed., *God and Evil* (Englewood Cliffs, N. J. : Prentice-Hall, 1964), 103–112.

16. Smart, "Omnipotence, Evil and Supermen," 107.

17. Farrer, *Love Almighty and Ills Unlimited*, 65–66.

18. See Hick, *Evil and the God of Love*, 245–253.

19. See Griffin, in Davis, ed., *Encountering Evil*, 53–54; see also Griffin's *God, Power and Evil* (Philadelphia: Westminster Press, 1976), 174–204.

20. Griffin, in Davis, ed., *Encountering Evil*, 53–54.

21. Griffin, in Davis, ed., *Encountering Evil*, 53.

22. Griffin, in Davis, ed., *Encountering Evil*, 53.

23. There is a growing literature concerned with the problem of animal suffering. For Hick's discussion, see *Evil and the God of Love*, 309–317, and his response to critics in Davis, ed., *Encountering Evil*, 68.

24. Hick, "An Irenaean Theodicy," 47.

25. Among Hick's numerous critics and defenders are the following: Rowland Puccetti, "The Loving God—Some Observations on John Hick's *Evil and the God of Love*," *The Philosophical Quarterly* (1964), 255–268; Peter Hare and Edward Madden, *Evil and the Concept of God* (Springfield, IL: C. C. Thomas, 1968); Stanley Kane, "The Failure of Soul-Making Theodicy," *International Journal for Philosophy of Religion* (1975), 1–22; Robert Mesle, "The Problem of Genuine Evil: A Critique of John Hick's Theodicy," *Journal of Religion* (1986), 412–430; Keith Ward, "Freedom and the Irenaean Theodicy," *Journal of Theological Studies* (1969), 249–254; Clement Dore, "An Examination of the 'Soul-Making' Theodicy," *American Philosophical Quarterly* (1970), 119–130; Terrence Tilley, "The Use and Abuse of Theodicy," *Horizons, Journal of the College Theology Society* (1984), 304–319; Terry R. Mathis, *Against John Hick* (Washington: University Press of America, 1985), 78–93; Griffin, *God, Power and Evil*, 174–204; and the critical comments

of Sontag, Davis, Griffin and Roth in Stephen Davis, ed., *Encountering Evil*.

· 26. See Hick's response to his critics (Griffin, Davis, Roth and Sontag) in Stephen Davis, ed., *Encountering Evil*, 63–68. See also his earlier response to both Augustinians (Catholic and Protestant) who claim that his theodicy is *theologically* unsound, and to skeptical or atheist philosophers who claim it is *philosophically* unsound: *Evil and the God of Love*, 372–384.

27. See, for example, Davis, in Davis, ed., *Encountering Evil*, 58–59.

28. Hick, "An Irenaean Theodicy," 49–50. See also *Evil and the God of Love*, 303–304.

29. See Hick, "An Irenaean Theodicy," 50.

30. Hick, "An Irenaean Theodicy," 51.

31. This is not necessarily the case, yet it does seem that maturity and spiritual qualities are gained through the overcoming of obstacles more so than if there were no such obstacles (were such a perfect world even possible).

32. Terrence Tilley, "The Use and Abuse of Theodicy," 312.

33. Sontag, for example, argues this point against Hick: see Davis, ed., *Encountering Evil*, 56.

34. Davis, in Davis, ed., *Encountering Evil*, 58. Hick's response is to concede what while it is "hard to determine whether the human race is improving, ethically or religiously, along the plane of earthly history . . . the postulated movement towards human perfection should occur in the personal histories and interactions of individuals through the successive pareschatological worlds" (66).

35. See, for example, Davis in Davis, ed., *Encountering Evil*, 59–61.

36. See, for example, John Rist, "Coherence and the God of Love," *Journal of Theological Studies* (1972), 95–105. Hick has responded in his article, "Coherence and the God of Love Again," *Journal of Theological Studies* (1973), 522–528. Another critic, Keith Ward, has argued that Hick's defense of human free will is invalid. See Ward, "Freedom and the Irenaean Theodicy," *Journal of Theological Studies* (1969), 249–254; and Hick's

response in his article, "Freedom and the Irenaean Theodicy Again," *Journal of Theological Studies* (1970), 419–422.

Chapter 6

1. See Charles Hartshorne, "A New Look at the Problem of Evil," in F. C. Dommeyer, ed., *Current Philosophical Issues: Essays in Honor of Curt John Ducasse* (Springfield: C. C. Thomas, 1966), 201–212.

2. Griffin's book, *God, Power, and Evil* (Philadelphia: Westminster, 1976), was the first full-length study of process theodicy. My own book, *Evil and the Process God* (New York: The Edwin Mellen Press, 1985), was designed to complement Griffin's: where Griffin is concerned to argue the case against classical theodicies and to propose a process theodicy, I have sought to uncover some of the inner tensions within process theism and to note the implications for process theodicy.

3. Charles Hartshorne, "Ideas and Theses of Process Philosophers," in Lewis Ford, ed., *Two Process Philosophers* (Tallahassee, FL: AAR Studies in Religion, 1973), 102.

4. Hartshorne, "A New Look at the Problem of Evil," 202.

5. Hartshorne, "A New Look at the Problem of Evil," 204.

6. Hartshorne, "A New Look at the Problem of Evil," 202.

7. See Hartshorne's book, *Omnipotence and Other Theological Mistakes* (Albany: SUNY Press, 1984).

8. Hartshorne, "A New Look at the Problem of Evil," 205.

9. See Griffin's *God, Power, and Evil.*

10. See Alfred North Whitehead's major work, *Process and Reality* (New York: Macmillan, 1929), 520. The corrected version, edited by David Griffin and D. W. Sherburne (New York: The Free Press, 1978), is more useful.

11. See Alfred North Whitehead, *Adventures of Ideas* (New York: Macmillan, 1933), 213.

12. Whitehead, for example, refers to the traditional Christian God as "the supreme agency of compulsion" (*Adventures of Ideas*, 213), while he describes the process God as the "absence of force" (*Religion in the Making* {New York: Macmillan,

1926}, 27). Hartshorne writes: "The divine method of world control is called 'persuasion' by Whitehead and is one of the greatest of all metaphysical discoveries." He contends that Whitehead's discovery "challenges comparison with the more traditional view . . . {which leaves unexplained} our knowledge that objects influence but do not coerce subjects" (*The Divine Relativity* {New Haven: Yale University Press, 1948}, 142). See my article, "Process Theism: Does a Persuasive God Coerce?" *Southern Journal of Philosophy* (1979), 133–143, and my book, *Evil and the Process God*. See also David Basinger's "Divine Persuasion: Could the Process God Do More?" *Journal of Religion* (1979), 332–347. See also Lewis Ford, *The Lure of God* (Philadelphia: Fortress, 1978); John Cobb and David Griffin, *Process Theology: An Introductory Exposition* (Philadelphia: Westminster Press, 1976); John Cobb, *God and the World* (Philadelphia: Westminster Press, 1969); etc.

13. Stephen Ely, *The Religious Availability of Whitehead's God* (Madison: University of Wisconsin Press, 1942).

14. Hick, in Davis, ed., *Encountering Evil* (Atlanta: John Knox Press, 1981), 122.

15. Sontag, in Davis, ed., *Encountering Evil*, 127.

16. Davis, in Davis, ed., *Encountering Evil*, 127.

17. See, for example, Hare and Madden's critique of the process position in their article, "Evil and Persuasive Power," *Process Studies* (1972), 44–48, and Dalton Baldwin's response, "Evil and Persuasive Power: A Response to Hare and Madden," *Process Studies* (1973), 250–272.

18. See Griffin, in Davis, ed., *Encountering Evil*, 54.

19. I have argued—as early as 1975 in my Ph.D. dissertation and in an article, "Process Theism: Does a Persuasive God Coerce?" *Southern Journal of Philosophy* (1979)—that process theists have not defended in a coherent and convincing manner the central tenet that God's causal activity is solely persuasive: see my 1985 book, *Evil and the Process God*, where this issue is discussed in direct relationship to the theodicy issue. See also my recent chapter, "Hartshorne and Theodicy," in R. Kane and S. Phillips, eds., *Charles Hartshorne, Process Theology and Religion* (Albany: SUNY Press, 1989), 55–71.

20. See, for example, Nancy Frankenberry, "Some Prob-

lems in Process Theodicy," *Religious Studies* (1982), 179–197.
Traditional theists find the supposed dichotomy between divine
persuasive and divine coercive power to be an inadequate and
condescending rhetoric.

21. See my *Evil and the Process God*, 68–70.

22. See my article, "Hartshorne's New Look at Theodicy,"
Studies in Religion (1979), 281–291.

23. See Hartshorne, *The Divine Relativity*, 142, etc.

24. See Hartshorne, *Man's Vision of God and the Logic of
Theism* (Chicago: Willett, Clark, 1941; reissued, Hamden, CT:
Archon Books, 1964), 30.

25. Hartshorne, *Man's Vision of God*, 30.

26. Hartshorne, *A Natural Theology for Our Time* (La Salle:
Open Court, 1967), 81.

27. Hartshorne, *Creative Synthesis and Philosophic Method*
(La Salle: Open Court, 1970), 237–238.

28. See Hartshorne's *Creative Synthesis*, 1.

29. Hartshorne, *Reality as Social Process* (Glencoe: Free
Press and Boston: Beacon Press, 1953; reprinted, New York: Haf-
ner Publishing Company, 1971), 107.

30. See, for example, the recent criticisms of Davis, in
Davis, ed., *Encountering Evil*, 126–127.

31. See, for example, Griffin, "Creation Out of Chaos and
the Problem of Evil," in Davis, ed., *Encountering Evil*, 101–102.
There are several metaphysical arguments in support of the rejection of the traditional doctrine of "creation out of nothing": see
my discussion of this point in *Evil and the Process God*, 85–87.

32. Griffin makes this point in "Creation Out of Chaos and
the Problem of Evil," 104–105.

33. See Griffin, in Davis, ed., *Encountering Evil*, 53–54.

34. See my *Evil and the Process God*, 85–87, etc.

35. In Whiteheadian terminology this is referred to as the
"Primordial" and the "Consequent" Natures of God; Hartshorne
prefers the terminology "abstract" and "concrete" aspects of God
to denote the same thing: God is the creative source of infinite
potential and yet also has a more concrete dimension which consists of all actualized potentialities. See his *The Divine Relativity*.

36. See, for example, Griffin's discussion in "Creation Out

of Chaos and the Problem of Evil," 106; and my *Evil and the Process God*, 142–167.

37. See Griffin, "Creation Out of Chaos and the Problem of Evil," 106–112, and his *God, Power and Evil*, 282–300.

38. Hartshorne, *Creative Synthesis*, 304.

39. Whitehead, *Process and Reality*, 161. See also Griffin, *God, Power and Evil*, 287.

40. The phrase is Whitehead's (*Process and Reality*, 532) and it is endorsed by other process writers.

41. Griffin argues, with Hartshorne, that God shares all our sufferings in a manner analogous to the way we share in the suffering of our bodies. God alone is in a position to judge whether the goods achievable are worth the suffering we must endure. See Griffin's "Creation Out of Chaos and the Problem of Evil," 110–111. See my discussion of this point in *Evil and the Process God*, 154–157.

42. Peter Hare and Edward Madden, "Evil and Unlimited Power," *Review of Metaphysics* (1966), 287.

43. Peter Hare and Edward Madden, *Evil and the Concept of God* (Springfield, IL: C. C. Thomas, 1968), 124.

44. John Hick, *Philosophy of Religion*, 3rd. ed. (Englewood Cliffs, N. J.: Prentice-Hall, 1983), 55.

45. Hick, *Philosophy of Religion*, 55. For the process theists' responses to this type of criticism, see my *Evil and the Process God*, 216–218.

46. See my discussion of this point in *Evil and the Process God*, 157–167. There is a growing process literature on this question of immortality: see, for example, David Griffin's "The Possibility of Subjective Immortality in Whitehead's Philosophy," *Modern Schoolman* (1975), 39–57; Lewis Ford and Marjorie Suchochi, "A Whiteheadian Reflection on Subjective Immortality," *Process Studies* (1977), 1–13; etc.

47. Hick's theodicy, as we have seen, depends upon an afterlife world; otherwise, it would be a cruel and vicious act of God to have created human beings in an imperfect way and such that we would not be able to reach a final fulfillment. Belief in an afterlife redemption has been a major aspect of the solution to

the theodicy puzzle since at least New Testament days. Nancy Frankenberry shares with many others a dissatisfaction with the lack of an eschatology in process theodicy (see her "Some Problems with Process Theodicy," 192–195). Davis likewise argues that the problem of evil cannot "be solved from a Christian perspective without crucial reference to the future" (in Davis, ed., *Encountering Evil*, 131).

48. See my *Evil and the Process God*, 222. See also my forthcoming article, co-authored with Norman King, "Hartshorne and Rahner on Death and Eternal Life," in *Horizons, Journal of the College Theology Society* (1988).

Chapter 7

1. See George Schlesinger, *Religion and the Scientific Method* (Dordrecht: Reidel, 1977); "The Problem of Evil and the Problem of Suffering," *American Philosophical Quarterly* (1964), 244–247; "Omnipotence and Evil: An Incoherent Problem," *Sophia* (1965), 21–24; "On the Possibility of the Best of All Possible Worlds," *Journal of Value Inquiry* (1970), 229–232; and "Suffering and Evil," in *Contemporary Philosophy of Religion*, Stephen M. Cahn and David Shatz, eds. (New York: O.U.P., 1982), 25–31.

2. Among Schlesinger's critics are the following: Thomas Morris, "A Response to the Problems of Evil," *The Journal of Philosophy* (1984), 173–185; Jay Rosenberg, "The Problem of Evil Revisited: A Reply to Schlesinger," *Journal of Value Inquiry* (1970), 212–218; Winslow Shea, "God, Evil, and Professor Schlesinger," *Journal of Value Inquiry* (1970), 219–228; George Walls, "Other Worlds and the Comparison of Value," *Sophia* (1979), 11–15; and John Feinberg, *Theologies and Evil* (Washington, D. C.: University Press of America, 1979), 86–94; etc.

3. The latter is the claim of Rosenberg, "The Problem of Evil Revisited," 218.

4. Schlesinger, "The Problem of Evil and the Problem of Suffering," 244.

5. Schlesinger, "The Problem of Evil and the Problem of Suffering," 246.

6. Schlesinger, "The Problem of Evil and the Problem of Suffering," 246.

7. Schlesinger, "The Problem of Evil and the Problem of Suffering," 246.

8. Schlesinger, "The Problem of Evil and the Problem of Suffering," 246.

9. Rosenberg, "The Problem of Evil Revisited," 216.

10. Rosenberg, "The Problem of Evil Revisited," 216–217. See also Morris' discussion of this type of criticism in his "A Response to the Problems of Evil," 180–182. See also Schlesinger's brief response to the criticisms of Shea and Rosenberg in his "On the Possibility of the Best of All Possible Worlds," 229–232.

11. Shea, "God, Evil, and Professor Schlesinger," 219–225.

12. Shea, "God, Evil, and Professor Schlesinger," 227.

13. Shea, "God, Evil, and Professor Schlesinger," 228. See also Schlesinger's response and especially the critical discussion by Feinberg, *Theologies and Evil*, 86–94.

14. See, for example, Plantinga's *God and Other Minds* (Ithaca and London: Cornell University Press, 1967, 115–155), *God, Freedom and Evil* (New York: Harper and Row, 1974), and *The Nature of Necessity* (Oxford: Clarendon, 1974). Among the critical studies of Plantinga's writings are the following: William Rowe, "God and Other Minds," *Nous* (1969), 259–284; Ingemar Hedenius, "Disproofs of God's Existence?" *Personalist* (1971), 23–43; Theodore Guleserian, "God and Possible Worlds: The Modal Problem of Evil," *Nous* (1983), 221–238; Steven Boer, "The Irrelevance of the Free Will Defence," *Analysis* (1978), 110–112; Robert McKim, "Worlds Without Evil," *International Journal for Philosophy of Religion* (1984), 161–170; Fred Chernoff, "The Obstinance of Evil," *Mind* (1980), 269–273; Wesley Morriston, "Is Plantinga's God Omnipotent?" *Sophia* (1984), 45–57; Antony Flew, "Compatibilism, Free Will and God," *Philosophy* (1973), 231–244; Barry Gan, "Plantinga's Transworld Depravity: It's Got Possibilities," *International Journal for Philosophy of Religion* (1982), 169–177; Richard Grigg, "Theism

and Proper Basicality: A Response to Plantinga," *International Journal for Philosophy of Religion* (1983), 123–127; James Sterba, "God, Plantinga and a Better World," *International Journal for Philosophy of Religion* (1976), 446–451; David and Randall Basinger, "Divine Omnipotence: Plantinga and Griffin," *Process Studies* (1981), 11–24; Hugh LaFollette, "Plantinga on the Free Will Defence," *International Journal for Philosophy of Religion* (1980), 123–132; Jonathan Evans, "LaFollette on Plantinga's Free Will Defence," *International Journal for Philosophy of Religion* (1983), 117–121; Susan Anderson, "Plantinga and the Free Will Defence," *Pacific Philosophical Quarterly* (1981), 274–281; David Basinger, "Anderson on Plantinga: A Response," *Philosophy Research Archives* (1983), 315–320; J.E. Barnhart, "Theodicy and the Free Will Defence: Response to Plantinga and Flew," *Religious Studies* (1977), 439–453; Wallace Murphree, "Can Theism Survive Without the Devil?" *Religious Studies* (1985), 231–244; Patrick Grim, "Plantinga's God and Other Monstrosities," *Religious Studies* (1979), 91–97; Robert Ackerman, "An Alternative Free Will Defence," *Religious Studies* (1982), 365–372; Nelson Pike, "Plantinga on Free Will and Evil," *Religious Studies* (1979), 449–473; Terrence Tilley, "The Use and Abuse of Theodicy," *Horizons* (1984), 304–319; Kenneth Surin, *Theology and the Problem of Evil* (Oxford: Blackwell, 1986), 70–78; etc.

15. Plantinga's response is in his "Self-Profile," in *Alvin Plantinga*, James E. Tomberlin and Peter Van Inwagen, eds. (Boston: Reidel, 1985), 45.

16. Plantinga, "Self-Profile," 45.

17. Plantinga," Self-Profile," 47.

18. Plantinga, "Self-Profile," 47. See David and Randall Basinger's article, "Divine Omnipotence: Plantinga and Griffin."

19. See Plantinga, *God, Freedom, and Evil*, 34–44, and *The Nature of Necessity*, 180–184.

20. See Tilley's discussion of this point in his "The Use and Abuse of Theodicy," 305–310.

21. See John Hick, *Evil and the God of Love*, second edition (New York: Harper and Row, 1978), 370.

22. Hick, *Evil and the God of Love*, 370.

23. See Plantinga, "The Probalistic Argument from Evil," *Philosophical Studies* (1979), 1–55. See also, "Self-Profile," 53–55.

24. Griffin, *God, Power, and Evil* (Philadelphia: Westminster Press, 1976), 272. Flew comments: "to make this more than just another desperate *ad hoc* expedient of apologetic it is necessary to produce independent reasons for launching such an hypothesis (if "hypothesis" is not too flattering a term for it)" (cited by Plantinga, in "Self-Profile," 43).

25. See, for example, "Self-Profile," 43.

26. David and Randall Basinger, "Divine Omnipotence: Plantinga vs Griffin," 20.

27. See Pike, "Plantinga on Free Will and Evil," *Religious Studies* (1979), 473.

28. Surin, *Theology and the Problem of Evil*, 74. See also Robert Ackerman, "An Alternative Free Will Defence," which argues that Plantinga's God cannot be reconciled with the biblical vision of divine agency.

29. See J. L. Mackie, "Omnipotence," *Sophia* (1962), 13–25; "Evil and Omnipotence," *Mind* (1955), 200–212, reprinted in Nelson Pike, ed., *God and Evil* (Englewood Cliffs, N. J.: Prentice-Hall, 1964), 153–158; "Theism and Utopia," *Philosophy* (1962), 153–158; and *The Miracle of Theism* (Oxford: Clarendon Press, 1982); Antony Flew, "Divine Omnipotence and Human Freedom" and "Theology and Falsification," in Antony Flew and Alasdair MacIntyre, eds., *New Essays in Philosophical Theology* (London: SCM Press, 1955), etc. There have been a plethora of responses to the writings of Mackie and Flew.

30. Mackie, "Evil and Omnipotence," 46–60.

31. Antony Flew, ed., *New Essays in Philosophical Theology*, 152. Flew's other classic argument against theistic belief, and in particular the problem of evil, is his famous falsification challenge. See his essay, "Theology and Falsification," and the responses of R.M. Hare, Basil Mitchell and I.M. Crombie, in Flew's edited volume, *New Essays in Philosophical Theology*, 96–130. Ian Barbour's response to this challenge is also very relevant

and one of the most persuasive; see Barbour's *Myths, Models, and Paradigms* (New York: Harper and Row, 1974), 126–133, etc.

32. See also Hick's response, in *Evil and the God of Love*, 269–271.

33. See, for example, Plantinga, *God, Freedom, and Evil*, 39–57.

34. For Swinburne's main writings on the topic see his *The Existence of God* (Oxford: Clarendon Press, 1979), 200–224; "Natural Evil," *American Philosophical Quarterly* (1978), 295–301; "The Problem of Evil," in *Reason and Religion*, Stuart Brown, ed. (Ithaca: Cornell University Press, 1977), 81–102; etc.

35. See, for example, the criticisms of Surin, *Theology and the Problem of Evil*, 78–86; Eleonore Stump, "Knowledge, Freedom and the Problem of Evil," *International Journal for Philosophy of Religion* (1983), 49–58; David O'Connor, "On Natural Evil's Being Necessary for Free Will," *Sophia* (1985), 36–44; David Acinar, "Swinburne on Natural Evil," *Religious Studies* (1983), 65–73; Bruce Wachterhauser, "The Problem of Evil and Moral Skepticism," *International Journal for Philosophy of Religion* (1985), 167–174; Paul Moser, "Natural Evil and the Free Will Defence," *International Journal for Philosophy of Religion* (1985), 167–174; etc.

36. See Bruce Reichenbach, "Natural Evils and Natural Laws: A Theodicy for Natural Evil," *International Philosophical Quarterly* (1976), 179–196; "The Inductive Argument from Evil," *American Philosophical Quarterly* (1980), 221–227; "The Deductive Argument from Evil," *Sophia* (1981); and especially his book, *Evil and a Good God* (New York: Fordham University Press, 1982). Austin Farrer's classic theodicy book, *Love Almighty and Ills Unlimited* (London: Collins, 1962) is also concerned with the question of natural evil. See the discussion of Farrer's theodicy in *Chapter 4*.

37. Swinburne, *The Existence of God*, 202–203.

38. Swinburne, *The Problem of Evil*, 207.

39. Swinburne, *The Existence of God*, 219.

40. Swinburne, *The Existence of God*, 219.

41. Swinburne, *The Existence of God*, 219.

42. See, for example, Surin, *Theology and the Problem of Evil*, 81.

43. Stump, "Knowledge, Freedom and the Problem of Evil," 52.

44. Acinar, "On Natural Evil's Being Necessary for Free Will," 39; see also his "Swinburne on Natural Evil."

45. See H. J. McCloskey, "God and Evil," *The Philosophical Quarterly* (1960), 97–114, reprinted in Nelson Pike, ed., *God and Evil* (Englewood Cliffs, N.J.: Prentice-Hall, 1964), 61–84; and his "The Problem of Evil," *The Journal of Bible and Religion* (1962), 187–197.

46. Reichenbach, *Evil and a Good God*, 103.

47. Reichenbach, *Evil and A Good God*, 103.

48. See Reichenbach, *Evil and a Good God*, 104–106.

49. Reichenbach, *Evil and a Good God*, 110.

50. Cited by Reichenbach, *Evil and a Good God*, 111, from F. R. Tennant, *Philosophical Theology, II* (Cambridge: Cambridge University Press, 1928), 199–200.

51. Reichenbach, *Evil and a Good God*, 111.

Chapter 8

1. Among Lewis' most important writings on theodicy, see *The Problem of Pain* (London: Collins, 1949) and *A Grief Observed* (New York: Bantam, 1963).

2. See John Beversluis, *C. S. Lewis and the Search for Rational Religion* (Grand Rapids, MI: Eerdmans, 1985), xi. Beversluis provides an updated bibliography of both Lewis' critics and supporters. Among the former are E. L. Allen, R. C. Churchill, Robert Eisler, Norman Pittenger, and Mary Scrutton. Among the latter are Corbin Scott Carnell, Richard Cunnigham, Margaret Hannay, Paul Holmer, Carolyn Keefe, Clyde Kilby, Peter Kreeft, Brian Murphy, Richard Purtill, and William Luther White. For bibliographical information on these writers, see Beversluis' notes on pages 168–170 of the aforementioned book.

3. See Beversluis, *C. S. Lewis*, xi.

4. Robert Wall, "The Problem of Pain Observed: A Study of C. S. Lewis on Suffering," *Journal of Evangelical Theological Studies*, 447.

5. Lewis, *The Problem of Pain*, 83.

6. Lewis, *The Problem of Pain*, 21.

7. See C. S. Lewis, *Miracles* (London: Fontana, 1947).

8. See Lewis, *Miracles*, 104–106.

9. Carl F. H. Henry, *God, Revelation and Authority* (Waco, TX: Word Books, 1983), 459. I am indebted to one of my former graduate students, Gene Templemeyer, for much of this discussion of conservative evangelical theology. His MA thesis, which I directed, is an extremely useful study of divine power in contemporary evangelical thinking (*A Persuasive God and Human Freedom: An Evangelical View*, University of Windsor, 1987).

10. Arthur Pink, *The Sovereignty of God* (London: The Banner of Truth Trust, 1961), 20–21.

11. Augustus Strong, *Systematic Theology* (Old Tappan, N.J.: Flemming Revell Co., 1976).

12. Andrew Rule, "Providence and Preservation," in Carl Henry, ed., *Basic Christian Doctrines: Contemporary Evangelical Thought* (New York: Holt, Rinehart and Winston, 1962).

13. J. I. Packer, *Knowing God* (London: Hodder and Stoughton, 1973).

14. Pink, *The Sovereignty of God*, 9. The majority view is represented by Strong's comment that "{h}uman freedom is not rendered impossible by divine omnipotence, but exists by virtue of it" (Strong, *Systematic Theology*, 288).

15. Templemeyer has documented this thesis very convincingly in his *A Persuasive God and Human Freedom*. See John Claypool, *Tracks of a Fellow Struggler* (New York: Pillar Books, 1976); Richard Foster, *Celebration of Discipline* (San Francisco: Harper and Row, 1978); Anthony Campola, *The Power Delusion* (Wheaton, IL: Victor Books, 1983); etc.

16. Harold S. Kushner, *When Bad Things Happen to Good People* (New York: Avon Books, 1981).

17. Kushner, *When Bad Things Happen to Good People*, 6.

18. Kushner, *When Bad Things Happen to Good People*, 23.

19. Kushner, *When Bad Things Happen to Good People*, 26.

20. Burton Z. Cooper, *Why God?* (Atlanta: John Knox, 1988), 71.

21. Kushner, *When Bad Things Happen to Good People*, 134.

22. The well-known Chicago theologian, Martin Marty, among others, has rejected Kushner's apparently weakened God: "To the degree that {God} is limited, he is on the same footing as all creatures, and thus it is pointless to call God, God." Chuck Colson, the former aide to Richard Nixon, speaking from a born-again, evangelical perspective, likewise complains that Kushner's God "isn't dead . . . just sick and feeble." For references, see the excellent discussion by Cooper in his book, *Why God?* 70–71.

23. Kushner, *When Bad Things Happen to Good People*, 47.

24. Kushner, *When Bad Things Happen to Good People*, 58.

25. Kushner, *When Bad Things Happen to Good People*, 81.

26. See Kushner, *When Bad Things Happen to Good People*, 132–148.

27. In an interview with process theologian John Cobb in 1984, Kushner admits that his position is very similar to that of process theodicists, with whom he had had no prior acquaintance. The interview, "Rabbi Harold S. Kushner, Interviewed by John Cobb," is available on audio and video tapes from the Interfaith Media Centre and the Centre for Process Studies (Claremont, CA).

28. Warren McWilliams, *The Passion of God* (Macon, GA: Mercer University Press, 1985). The discussion in this book focuses upon Moltmann, Cone, MacGreggor, Kitamori, D. D. Williams, and Jung Lee.

29. Richard Bauckham, "'Only the Suffering God Can Help': Divine Passibility in Modern Theology," *Themelios* (1984), 6.

30. Ronald Goetz, "The Suffering God: The Rise of a New Orthodoxy," *The Christian Century* (1986), 385.

31. H.M. Relton, *Studies in Christian Doctrine* (London: Macmillan, 1960), the cited text first being published in the *Church Quarterly Review* in 1917. See Bauckham's article (note 29) for a useful and informative documentation of this point.

32. J.K. Mozley, *The Impassibility of God: A Survey of Christian Thought* (London: Cambridge University Press, 1926).

33. Nicholas Berdyaev, *The Meaning of History* (London: Geoffrey Bles, 1939); Kazoh Kitamori, *Theology and the Pain of God* (London: SCM Press, 1966).

34. See Schilling, *God and Human Anguish* (Nashville: Abingdon, 1977), 251.

35. See, for example, Warren McWilliams, *The Passion of God.* See also the article by Ronald Goetz, "The Suffering God: Rise of a New Orthodoxy," 385–389.

36. See Terrence E. Fretheim, *The Suffering God: An Old Testament Perspective* (Philadelphia: Fortress, 1984).

37. Claus Westermann, *Elements in Old Testament Theology*, trans., Douglas W. Scott (Atlanta: John Knox Press, 1982), 138–149.

38. Abraham Heschel, *The Prophets* (New York: Harper and Row, 1962), 241.

39. Heschel, *The Prophets*, 257. See Bauckham's excellent discussion of this point in his "Only the Suffering God Can Help," 9.

40. Lewis S. Ford, *The Lure of God: A Biblical Background for Process Theism* (Philadelphia: Fortress, 1978).

41. Daniel Day Williams has suggested at least three reasons for the rise in popularity of the doctrine of divine suffering: (1) process theology; (2) the biblical theology movement which flourished during the Second World War (which saw God as an active participant in human history); and (3) contemporary understandings of the atonement (the passion of Christ has been taken more seriously as the model for God). See his puissant book, *What Present Day Theologians Are Thinking* (New York: Harper and Row, 1967), 171–172. See also Schilling's insightful chapter on this issue and its development, in his *God and Human Anguish*, 235–260.

42. Richard Bauckham, "'Only the Suffering God Can Help': Divine Passibility in Modern Theology," 9.

43. Goetz, "The Suffering God," 388.

44. Goetz, "The Suffering God," 388.

45. Moltmann, *The Crucified God*, 46.

46. Jürgen Moltmann, *The Church in the Power of the Spirit: A Contribution to Messianic Ecclesiology* (London: SCM Press, 1977), 64.

47. Schilling, *God and Human Anguish*, 258.

Chapter 9

1. Moses Mendelssohn, *Jerusalem and Other Writings*, translated and edited by Alfred Jospe (New York: Schocken Books, 1969), 68.

2. Richard Rubenstein, *After Auschwitz* (Indianapolis: Bobbs-Merrill, 1968).

3. Rubenstein, *After Auschwitz*, 153. Elsewhere, he writes: "There is simply no way to harmonize Auschwitz with the Biblical God who is the omnipotent judge of the world and the ultimate author of human history" ("Homeland and Holocaust," in *Religious Situation*, Donald Cutler, ed. {Boston: Beacon Press, 1968}, 42).

4. Rubenstein, *After Auschwitz*, 86–87.

5. See Donald Burt, "The Powerlessness of God or the Powerlessness of Man," in *The Existence of God*, Proceedings of the American Catholic Philosophical Association, Volume 46, George F. McLean, ed. (Washington, D.C.: Catholic University of America, 1972).

6. See S. Daniel Breslauer, "Theodicy and Ethics: Post-Holocaust Reflection," *American Journal of Theology and Philosophy* (1987), 141.

7. See Eliezer Berkovits, *Faith After the Holocaust* (New York: Ktav Publishing House, 1973).

8. Berkovitis, *Faith After the Holocaust*, 127.

9. See Emil Fackenheim, *The Jewish Return into History* (New York: Harper and Row, 1978), and his *God's Presence in History: Jewish Affirmations and Philosophical Reflections* (New York: Harper and Row, 1970).

10. Arthur A. Cohen, *The Tremendum: A Theological Interpretation of the Holocaust* (New York: Crossroad, 1981).

11. Maurice Friedman, *The Hidden Human Image* (New York: Dell, 1974).

12. Irving Greenberg, "Clouds of Smoke, Pillar of Fire: Judaism, Christianity, and Modernity after the Holocaust," in *Auschwitz: Beginning of a New Era? Reflections on the Holocaust*, Eva Fleschner, ed. (New York: Ktav Publishing House, 1977), 7–55.

13. See Immanuel Hartom, in *Encountering the Holocaust*, Byron Sherwin and Susan Ament, eds. (Chicago: Impact Press, 1979), 409.

14. See Rabbi Joel Teitelbaum, in *Encountering the Holocaust*, Sherwin and Ament, eds., 409.

15. See Ignaz Maybaum, in *Encountering the Holocaust*, Sherwin and Ament, eds., 409.

16. Martin Buber, *The Prophetic Faith* (New York: Harper and Row, 1949).

17. Ignatz Maybaum, *The Face of God After Auschwitz* (Amsterdam: Poink and Van Gennep, 1965).

18. Elie Wiesel, *Night* (New York: Avon Books, 1969). There are numerous studies of Wiesel's provocative thought: see, in particular, Robert McAfee Brown's *Elie Wiesel: Messenger to All Humanity* (Notre Dame: University of Notre Dame Press, 1983).

19. Abraham Joshua Heschel, "The Divine Pathos: The Basic Category of Prophetic Theology," *Judaism* (1953), 61–67.

20. Jonas, "The Concept of God after Auschwitz," *The Journal of Religion* (1987), 3.

21. Jonas, "The Concept of God After Auschwitz," 8–10.

22. Jonas, "The Concept of God After Auschwitz," 10–11.

23. See, for example, the argument of Michael Peterson, in his *Evil and the Christian God* (Grand Rapids, MI: Baker Book House, 1982).

24. Cited by John Hick, in his *Evil and the God of Love*, second edition (New York: Harper and Row, 1978), 310.

25. See Peter Singer, *Animal Liberation* (New York: Avon Books, 1977), and his chapter, "All Animals Are Equal," in T. Regan and P. Singer, eds., *Animal Rights and Human Obligations* (Englewood Cliffs, N.J.: Prentice-Hall, 1976). For references to Regan's writings, and those of others, see note 26.

26. For the arguments, supportive and critical, see, for

example: Jan Narveson, "Animal Rights," *Canadian Journal of Philosophy* (1977), 161–78; Tom Regan, "Narveson on Egoism and the Rights of Animals," *Canadian Journal of Philosophy* (1977), 179–186; Tom Regan, "The Moral Basis of Vegetarianism," *Canadian Journal of Philosophy* (1975), 181–214; Philip Devine, "The Moral Basis of Vegetarianism," *Philosophy* (1978), 481–505; Donald Vandeveer, "Animal Suffering," *Canadian Journal of Philosophy* (1980), 463–471; Roslind Godlovitch, "Animals and Morals," *Philosophy* (1971), 23–33; Frederick Ferré, "Theodicy and the Status of Animals," *American Philosophical Quarterly* (1986); George Wall, *Is God Really Good?: Conversations with a Theodicist* (Lanham, MD: University Press of America, 1983); C.E.M. Joad, "The Pains of Animals: A Problem in Theology," in C. S. Lewis, *God of the Dock: Essays on Theology and Ethics* (Grand Rapids, MI: Eerdmans, 1970), Chapter 20; Mary Midgley, *Animals and Why They Matter* (New York: Penguin Books, 1983); Michael Fox, "Animal Suffering and Rights: A Reply to Singer and Regan," *Ethics* (1978),134–139; G. Frey, "Animal Rights," *Analysis* (1977), 186–189; Stephen Clark, "Animal Wrongs," *Analysis* (1978), 147–149; Leslie Pickering Francis and Richard Norman, "Some Animals Are More Equal Than Others," *Philosophy* (1978), 507–527; Tibor Machan, "Some Doubts about Animal Rights,"*Journal of Value Inquiry* (1985), 73–75; etc.

27. Hick, *Evil and the God of Love*, 316. See, for example, Sontag's critique, in Stephen Davis, ed., *Encountering Evil* (Atlanta: John Knox Press, 1981), 56–57.

28. Hick, *Evil and the God of Love*, 313.

29. Hick, *Evil and the God of Love*, 314–315.

30. See C. S. Lewis, *The Problem of Pain* (London: Collins, 1941), 117–131.

31. See Hick, "An Irenaean Theodicy," in Davis, ed., *Encountering Evil*, 68.

32. See, for example, Harvey D. Egan, *What Are They Saying About Mysticism?* (New York: Paulist Press, 1982); Wayne Proudfoot, *Religious Experience* (Berkeley: University of California Press, 1985).

33. The question of "faith healing" certainly is relevant to the theodicy question, but it is an enormously complex issue which cannot be done justice here. The role of faith in the process of healing is being studied by psychologists and theologians alike, and while there appears to be evidence that a positive attitude and active faith aids in healing, the proper theological context of this issue is the debate about miracles and the complex issue as to how, exactly, God acts in the world. Norman Vincent Peale's celebrated book, *The Power of Positive Thinking* (New York: Fawcett Crest, 1952), is one of the best known of the myriad of books on inner human potential, selling well over three million copies. Other books include: Norman Cousins' *Anatomy of an Illness* (New York: Bantam, 1979) and *The Healing Heart* (New York: W.W. Norton and Co., 1983); Paul H. Wender and Donald F. Klein, *Mind, Mood and Medicine* (New York: Farrar, Straus, Giroux, 1981); Steven Locke and Douglas Colligan, *The Healer Within* (New York: New American Library, 1986); John Sanford, *Healing and Wholeness* (New York: Paulist Press, 1977); Kenneth Pelletier, *Mind as Healer, Mind as Slayer* (New York: Dell Publishing Co., 1977); J. Harold Ellens, *God's Grace and Human Health* (Nashville: Abingdon, 1982); etc.

34. To expect God to intervene by violating the laws which God has created would appear tantamount to implying that God was not capable of creating suitable laws in the first place. This, however, would suggest that God is less than perfect and in effect deny God's very nature as perfection. To expect, moreover, that God intervene intermittently to cure some particular illnesses or to prevent some disasters seems to be a matter of pure arbitrariness. If God can cure one case of cancer, then why not all cases of cancer? And if cancer is eradicated, then why not AIDS, and indeed all other diseases; and then why not all the inconveniences which human beings must endure? For a discussion of this point, see my *Evil and the Process God* (New York: Edwin Mellen Press, 1985), 124–128.

35. For discussions of miracles, see Ernst and Marie-Luise Keller, *Miracles in Dispute* (Philadelphia: Fortress, 1969); H.J. Richards, *The Miracles of Jesus* (Mystic, CT: Twenty-Third Pub-

lications, 1986); Robert Larmer, *Water into Wine: An Investigation of the Concept of Miracle* (Kingston and Montreal: McGill-Queens University Press, 1988); Colin Brown, *Miracles and the Critical Mind* (Grand Rapids, MI: Eerdmans, 1984); C.S. Lewis, *Miracles* (London: Fontana, 1947); etc.

A Selected
Annotated Bibliography

Archer, Gleason. *The Book of Job* (Grand Rapids, MI: Baker Book House, 1982).
  A useful commentary, intended for non-specialists, about the Book of Job's classic treatment of the theodicy issue.

Aufrecht, Walter, ed. *Studies in the Book of Job* (Waterloo, Ontario: Canadian Corporation for the Study of Religion, 1985).
  One of a myriad of books on Job, but one of the best. It is intended for scholars and includes a useful chapter on current trends in the study of the Book of Job.

Beversluis, John. *C. S. Lewis and the Search for Rational Religion* (Grand Rapids, MI: Eerdmans, 1985).
  A systematic and careful study of the thought of C. S. Lewis, which incorporates a critical analysis of his theodicy. One of the best of the innumerable books about Lewis.

Bowker, John. *Problems of Suffering in Religions of the World* (Cambridge: Cambridge University Press, 1970).

One of the most competent overviews of the problem of evil from the perspective not just of Christianity and Judaism, but also of Hinduism, Buddhism, Islam, Marxism, and others.

Carson, D. A. *Divine Sovereignty and Human Responsibility* (Atlanta: John Knox Press, 1981).
This book is a major achievement, showing clearly that the Bible is ambivalent concerning the relationship between divine power and human responsibility.

Crenshaw, James. *A Whirlpool of Torment* (Philadelphia: Fortress Press, 1984).
A scholarly study of various Old Testament texts, showing that the divine presence was often perceived in a negative way.

Crenshaw, James, ed., *Theodicy in the Old Testament* (Philadelphia: Westminster Press, 1983).
One of the few critical studies which addresses the theodicy question from a biblical perspective directly. It contains scholarly essays by major figures, from Walter Eichrodt (1934) to Klaus Koch (1950) and James Crenshaw (1975).

Davis, Stephen, ed., *Encountering Evil* (Atlanta: John Knox Press, 1981).
This anthology is one of the most useful and most highly recommended books on theodicy: it contains individual chapters by Hick, Griffin, Davis, Roth, and Sontag, and includes an informative critical dialogue among the five scholars.

Farrer, Austin. *Love Almighty and Ills Unlimited* (London: Collins, 1962, 1966).

An important and influential contemporary theodicy which focuses upon the problem of natural evil. The book does not consider the problem of moral evil, despite Farrer's important independent work on the free will issue.

Ford, Lewis. *The Lure of God: A Biblical Background for Process Theism* (Philadelphia: Fortress Press, 1978).

A major accomplishment by one of the most influential of contemporary process theists. The book uncovers the basis for an understanding of God as a persuasive power in biblical writings.

Galligan, Michael. *God and Evil* (New York: Paulist Press, 1976).

A critique of the "two major types of theodicies," the theodicy of free will and the theodicy of development, with useful references to many of the leading historical and contemporary theodicists.

Gerstenberger, E. S. and Schrage, W. *Suffering* (Nashville: Abingdon Press, 1977).

This book is indispensable as one of the most detailed studies of theodicy in the Old Testament (Gerstenberger) and the New Testament (Schrage). It lacks an overall view, however, and a serious consideration of how the biblical writings on God and suffering are relevant today.

Griffin, David. *God, Power and Evil* (Philadelphia: Westminster Press, 1976).

The first book-length study of theodicy from the perspective of process theology. It contains not only its author's process theodicy but detailed critiques of the more traditional theodicies of Augustine, Aquinas, Luther, Calvin, Leibniz, Barth, and others.

Hare, Peter and Madden, Edward. *Evil and the Concept of God* (Springfield, IL: Charles C. Thomas, 1968).
A significant critique of the major solutions to the theodicy issue proposed by various thinkers, historical and contemporary.

Hartshorne, Charles. "A New Look at the Problem of Evil," in F. C. Dommeyer, ed. *Current Philosophical Issues: Essays in Honor of Curt John Ducasse* (Springfield, IL: Charles C. Thomas, 1966).
A proposed solution of the theodicy issue by the world's most eminent of living process theists. The article focuses mainly upon the free will defense, ignoring other important aspects of Hartshorne's theodicy.

Hick, John. *Evil and the God of Love,* second edition (New York: Harper and Row, 1978).
This book has revived interest in the theodicy question. Hick presents a detailed examination of the traditional (Augustinian) theodicy and contrasts it with a thorough account of his alternative "Irenaean" theodicy.

Kushner, Harold. *When Bad Things Happen to Good People* (New York: Avon Books, 1981).
This book has become a best seller and has contributed immensely to a renewed interest in the problem of suffering among laypeople. It proposes a view of God as

less than all-powerful, yet offers little by way of an alternative.

Lewis, C. S. *A Grief Observed.* (New York: Bantam, 1976). Written after the tragic death of his wife, this book is an account of the grief Lewis endured and his questioning of God's love and power, culminating in a faith which became more mature and informed.

Lewis, C. S. *The Problem of Pain* (London: Collins, 1940). Lewis' classic statement on the problem of suffering, criticized by many as too conservative. His writings have had great influence among non-professional theologians.

Mackie, John. *The Miracle of Theism* (Oxford: Clarendon Press, 1982). Mackie's discussion of arguments for and against God's existence, from his skeptical perspective. The book's chapter on theodicy contains reference to Mackie's now famous "paradox of omnipotence."

Maritain, Jacques. *Saint Thomas and the Problem of Evil* (Milwaukee: Marquette University Press, 1942). Maritain, an influential Catholic theologian, discusses in this short book (the Aquinas Lectures) the theodicy of Saint Thomas Aquinas, focusing upon the meaning of evil and the question of free will.

Maritain, Jacques. *God and the Permission of Evil* (Milwaukee: The Bruce Publishing Company, 1966). This complex and scholarly book is Maritain's clearest statement on the theodicy issue, focusing upon moral evil (sin) and its relationship to God.

McWilliams, Warren, *The Passion of God* (Macon, GA: Mercer University Press, 1985).

This book discusses the thought of six contemporary thinkers, all of whom have focused upon the suffering of God: Moltmann, James Cone, Geddes MacGreggor, Kitamore, D. D. Williams, and Jung Young Lee. The implications for theodicy of the divine suffering theme are explored.

Moltmann, Jürgen. *The Crucified God* (New York: Harper and Row, 1974).

This is one of the best known and much discussed presentations of the suffering of God, and its implications for theodicy.

Oates, Wayne and Charles. *People in Pain: Guidelines for Pastoral Care* (Philadelphia: Westminster Press, 1986).

One of the best among the numerous books dealing with the existential (coping) dimension of suffering.

Peterson, Michael. *Evil and the Christian God* (Grand Rapids, MI: Baker Book House, 1982).

A reflective study of the theodicy issue, with reference to the theoretical and evidential problems and special reference to the problem of gratuitous evil.

Pike, Nelson, ed. *God and Evil* (Englewood Cliffs, N. J. : Prentice-Hall, 1964).

This short book is a valuable anthology of some of the major writings on theology, with selections from Dostoevski, David Hume and John Stuart Mill, to contemporary philosophers, Mackie, McCloskey, Pike and Ninian Smart.

Plantinga, Alvin. *God, Freedom, and Evil* (New York: Harper and Row, 1974).

Plantinga's influential free will defense is presented in detail, followed by a consideration of the traditional proofs for God's existence.

Rahner, Karl. "Why Does God Allow Us to Suffer?" *Theological Investigations, XIX* (New York: Crossroad, 1983), 194–208.

This is Rahner's clearest and most direct statement of the theodicy problem. He rejects the predominant traditional solutions and appeals to faith in the incomprehensibility of God as the ultimate solution.

Reichenbach, Bruce. *Evil and a Good God* (New York: Fordham University Press, 1982).

In this scholarly study, Reichenbach offers arguments against the common atheistic claim that natural evils are sufficient grounds for rejecting belief in God.

Schilling, P. A. *God and Human Anguish* (Nashville: Abingdon Press, 1977).

This is one of the most readable and insightful of books on the theodicy problem, replete with helpful illustrations. The book, unfortunately, is out of print.

Schlesinger, George. *Religion and the Scientific Method* (Dordrecht: Reidel, 1977).

One of the most important books on theodicy and one which makes the controversial claim that the problem can be resolved. Schlesinger contends that the amount of evil in the world does not argue conclusively against God's existence.

Simundson, Daniel. *Faith Under Fire* (Minneapolis: Augsburg, 1980).

> One of the most readable of the books concerned with biblical writings on theodicy. Simundson includes a useful analysis of the Book of Job and defines clearly "what is new in the New Testament" about the problem of evil.

Surin, Kenneth. *Theology and the Problem of Evil* (Oxford: Blackwell, 1986).

> An extraordinarily useful book, dealing with both the practical and the theoretical problems of evil, with ample references to the leading writers.

Swinburne, Richard. *The Existence of God* (Oxford: Clarendon Press, 1979).

> A technical examination of the arguments for and against God's existence. The chapter on the problem of evil contends that natural evils are necessary for there to be a meaningful human freedom.

Whitney, Barry. *Evil and the Process God* (New York: Edwin Mellen Press, 1985).

> A study of Hartshorne's process theodicy, finding that the definition of divine power in process theism as solely persuasive is problematic. The book also contains a survey of biblical and historical theodicies.

Other Books in this Series

5-0012
5-11

5147-5
5-11

5-147-5
5-11